Magic in the World

The Seven Laws
of
The Soul

By Donna Mitchell-Moniak

Llumina Press

Copyright Donna Mitchell-Moniak 2002

All rights reserved. No part of this publication may be reproduced or transmitted in any form or by any means, electronic or mechanical, including photocopy, recording, or any information storage and retrieval system, without permission in writing from the copyright owner. It is not to be duplicated or performed without the written consent of the author and the publisher.

Requests for permission to make copies of any part of this work should be mailed to Permissions Department, Llumina Press, PO Box 772246, Coral Springs, FL 33077-2246

ISBN: 1-932047-02-6

Printed in the United States of America

Contents

First Thoughts
Chapter one: Self-Actualization, Initiation, and Hierarchy
Chapter two: The Law of Sacrifice
Chapter three: The Law of Magnetic Impulse
Chapter four: The Law of Service
Chapter five: The Law of Repulse
Chapter six: The Law of Group Progress
Chapter seven: The Law of Expansive Response
Chapter eight: The Law of The Lower Four
Parting Thoughts
Glossary
Appendices
Bibliography

Dedicated to the Work and the Workers all over the world.
In humility, offered to the Master as a small piece of the Work.

Grateful acknowledgements to my husband, Steve, and daughters Alicia and Tracy for their love and support. To Jennifer Rick and Lee Le Beau for the first mark-up. To my co-workers Sara and Eva for their companionship. To Nan Lansdowne for her editorial comments. And to all the students for the inspiration I receive watching them grow.

Wisdom 9: 13 –18

"What man indeed can know the intentions of God?
Who can divine the will of the Lord?
The reasonings of mortals are unsure and our intentions unstable;
for a perishable body presses down the soul,
and this tent of clay weighs down the teeming mind.
It is hard enough for us to work out what is on earth,
laborious to know what lies within our reach;
Who then, can discover what is in the heavens?
As for your intention, who could have learnt it,
had you not granted Wisdom and sent your holy spirit from above?
Thus have the paths of those on earth been straightened
and men been taught what pleases you, and saved, by Wisdom."

First Thoughts

We light incense and perfumed smoke rises to the heavens, bringing with it our hopes, fears, aspirations, and dedications. The smoke blends with all the other scents, winds, and cross currents that it contacts and flavored now by all it has passed through, no longer remains just incense smoke. The Native Peoples understand that all must return to the Unmanifest Being from which all proceeded. That is why they purify themselves and clear the space around them with smoke before they enter into ceremony or prayer.

We light the light of life every time we incarnate into matter. The flame that flickers is the light of soul, not only our soul light but the light of every other living being, creature, and thing on this planet. The veiled light that is an individual will shine and glow only if given the opportunity. Otherwise, it will be dimmed like a candle put under a basket.

Among the many spiritual teachings given to humanity are simple teachings helping us live soul. Christ told us to let our light shine. In our shining we shall become the peacemakers, the merciful, and the truly righteous. By our shining, requiring faith born of knowing, we can move mountains, part rivers, feed many, and know the splendid harmony of life lived lovingly.

Buddha told us to disengage from the wants and worries of the world because our soul was slowly being bound like a slave to self-made shackles chaining us to the wheel of rebirth and suffering. Buddha saw the light of Life in all of its forms, saw that shackles and chains of desire tie us to that which is alluring, selfish and unlasting. He understood that only in freedom from these could we enter into liberation and light.

Patanjali, gave us the precepts of Raja Yoga, and offered a method of disengagement and living in a way true to soul's fullness. The Eight Means to Yoga speak clearly of right living, of orientation to the source of All Life, and of being clear with the self.

Yet underlying all of these teachings are the Seven Laws of the Soul. Each of these teachers spoke of the soul and its relationship with its Source, God, and to everything else that shares the spark of life divine. Each helped us recognize that we are soul, that we are just as capable as they of arriving at that point of life-knowing and living that is radiance itself. Each lived their teachings, shining for humanity, and for all the kingdoms of the world. Furthermore, each great teacher, each soul conscious person through history, and each and every person who lives is part of the great webwork, the iridescent tapestry that is the result of the principles underlying the laws of the soul.

What is Soul?

Soul is the light within each of us. It is consciousness, knowing, and being. Soul is the good, true, and beautiful that each person seeks to live or bring into the world. It is the whole that we long for. It is the whole that we are.

Soul is love and compassion, uplifting everything it touches, touching everything it can. Soul is the power of light, transforming, reforming, and making all things new.

Having said all of this, has anything been said? There are two tacks to take regarding soul, one is the personal, the other is the universal. The personal brings discussions of "my soul," "the soul," "your soul," "lost souls," and the like. This idea of soul is limited to our ideas of ourselves. In fact, the idea of a personal soul, is very much the idea of the psyche, offered by Pythagoras thousands of years ago and taken up by Plato, his student. The soul, in this case, is that which grows in awareness. It is what yearns, discovers, suffers, and lives joy. This soul is the one that incarnates, lifetime after lifetime. In the Christian model, it is the soul that goes to heaven (or elsewhere); in the Buddhist model, the soul moves through the bardo states upon death until it reaches a state of stasis; and in the Native American model, the soul becomes an ancestor, a teacher whose presence is available through prayer, remembrance, and ceremony.

The soul is given the opportunity to learn about itself, the world, and how life is one great whole.

Then there is Soul, not the soul, or my soul. Just Soul. This is the light divine within each person and everything else that exists. This is the presence of Life wherever it is found, regardless of form or state. Soul is that which binds life into a manifestation, conveys the design of that manifestation, and knows that it is good. Soul "was in the beginning" and was with God. Soul is the rhyme and reason for everything and illuminates that. Then, soul is the mystery of cosmos, its exactitude as well as its apparent chaos. Soul is what makes everything tick, and tick the way it does.

As we proceed, what, how, and why soul is will become clearer.

The Seven Laws of the Soul

The Seven Laws of the Soul, offered in *Esoteric Psychology, Vol. II* by Alice A. Bailey, are the edicts declaring the ways soul utilizes matter. We are matter. Our lives are matter. Our karma is matter. The substance of our everyday existence is all that soul has to work with, all that it has a chance to spiritualize. The work-a-day world, the business world, the family world, and all the worlds within each person are the places where soul tries to do its work. Many things militate against soul's success - our ignorance, attachments, fears, and our inertia - but soul has three very powerful things on its side. They are time, understanding, and love.

The seven laws of the soul use these three with deliberation and artistry. Via time and the law of rebirth we cannot escape the inevitability of heightened consciousness and the lessons required along the way. Through time we evolve, and grow better, as human beings, nations, as a kingdom, and as a planet. Time holds us, letting us leap only so far, fall so far, and grow so far. Then we do it again and again, each time perfecting a part of the self. In time we learn relativity, perspective, limitation and release. As we move with the laws of the soul and learn to incorporate the fullness of what they impart, we learn that time is not only the linear trap we have fought for so long, but that it is a permeable membrane with contours that flex. Empowered with the light of soul, time becomes a tool for the organization of all that needs be done as soul works its divine alchemy.

Understanding is used by the soul; equally understanding is what is gained. Soul moves with and in understanding. It knows exactly what it is doing, as opposed to the personality that is usually moving, talking, thinking, and emoting, but not fully aware why. Through understanding we learn to move with time as it teaches us. We learn to notice the small, unrecognized lessons, gestures, smiles and opportunities that continually present themselves. In growing degrees of understanding we learn the differences between reaction and response, conscious thought and mind turnings, compassion and passion. The more we understand the more we become aware of how much more there is to understand. Then we feel the love of soul.

Patient, humble, altruistic, and supremely powerful, the love of soul lies behind all outer events, regardless of what *personality*[1] thinks. The plans of the soul quietly work out through the veils of each day. These plans are likely basic and the intentions simple. They might be creating ways in which the personality will learn greater harmlessness or acceptance. Control, selflessness, right use of the emotions or the mind, or even acknowledgment of the importance of the body - any of these could be the plan of the soul for a given incarnation. In love and wisdom the soul works, steadfast and true to its intentions. The soul supports us in the process of managing the karma and the relationships in which we find ourselves. The love of soul is such that our noticing this support and management is not important; our movement through the process, however, is.

The Seven Laws of the Soul are our life-line, our anchor, and our destination, for we are destined to know our relatedness to all of life, to be The Divine Alchemists, and the Mighty Liberators. We are destined to inform matter (bring consciousness into form), and thereby release it and ourselves from the darkness of unconscious sleep. And we are destined to return, drawing all humanity, all kingdoms, all lives up with us into the fiery light supernal; for that light is our essence. It was our beginning, is our destination, as well as our true state of being.

The Seven Laws of the Soul are our assurance that matter will know consciousness. They are the matrix for all evolution. They are for all time because they are the ways by which consciousness itself grows and glows, magnetizes, radiates, liberates, and is itself set free.

The seven laws are not only the ways in which soul touches all matters of life, but are the principles behind the highest expression of soul. As we look out to the world we will see that the first four laws are available to

---

[1] Personality is the sense of unique self derived from our minds, emotions, and physical sensing of reality.

anyone working with the awareness of matter, on a level commensurate with their consciousness. With these laws soul not only touches matter but can be seen changing it. Examples will be given that will illumine how very basic the work of soul is in the personal life of any individual and in the collective life of humanity. The last three laws, however, bring us into the realms of subjective reality where soul becomes the conscious instrument of the *spirit*[2], that which birthed or breathed the soul into existence[3]. As a result we find that these last laws deal almost exclusively with groups or systems great and small.

The first four laws have their correspondence in the *three worlds of human endeavor*[4] (mental, emotional, and physical world) and in that which coordinates them, the personality, thus making four. Yet it should be kept in mind that these are laws of the soul, not laws of the personality or its vehicles. As a soul affects matter, it affects all forms of matter and all manner of substances. That is the great alchemical process that spiritualizes matter and materializes spirit. The last three laws require not only soul consciousness but that which is greater. The last three laws deal with the Spirit Self (*Monad*[5]) and the *three worlds of spiritual endeavor*[6].

Lenses – The Better to See With

To better understand these laws we will look through certain lenses.
1. The Alice Bailey work recognizes subjective groupings within humanity. Three primary ones are: the masses, disciples, and initiates.

---

[2] Spirit is the source, related to God, to the Life principle. Spirit is before, beyond, and greater than soul. Spoken of here, this is not the animating spirit of something, but its origin and eventual dissolution.
[3] Soul, then, is the outbreath of the Divine.
[4] The term three worlds of human endeavor or "the three worlds" will be used often. These worlds are the realm of human emotions/sentiency/desire, the realm of human thought/dream/illusion/analysis/conjecture, and the realm of physical plane existence determined by the five senses and that which they make known and experienced.
[5] Monad means one. In this case, the One is the original identity before time, before soul. It is spirit realized.
[6] The three worlds of spiritual endeavor are collectively named the Triad. Singly they are: manas/mind, buddhi/lighted reason, and atma/spiritual law.

a. The masses, are the general public, mostly unawakened but usually well meaning.
b. The disciples of the world are those who have woken up to life. These people aspire to soul, God, truth, and to assist their fellow brothers and sisters. They may participate in organized religion, or live a spiritual life of their own creation, or live a secular demonstration of the principles of shared existence in the world. Disciples are in all walks of life, and help to change the world from within. They are far from perfect, but they are more aware than their mass brothers and sisters.
c. The initiates. This third group is comprised of people who live in soul light. They move from the realms of meaning and causes into the worlds of illusion and effect that are the daily worlds. They illumine, they teach, they use power. Their relation in and with soul is never in question.

2. The ray energy that sub-stands the principle of the particular law will be discussed. The Seven Rays are the essence, the ingredients, the coloration, and the vibration of everything. They are the breaths of God, they are the children of the Divine Mother, they are the building blocks of life. Everything and everybody, today, tomorrow, and in the past are composites of the rays. The Rays govern all systems cyclically, be they star systems, planetary systems, kingdoms, or within a human being. Everything is here and is manifesting because of the Rays. The ray of the law of the soul will be one of the primary seven rays.

3. Another tool for understanding the laws will be the chakra system. The chakras or energy centers are the vortices through which forces move in us. There are seven primary centers found along the spine. There are many other lesser chakras, for instance in the feet and hands. Unknown by most people, unsensed, and yet always at work, the chakras put us in contact with one another, one part of

the self with another part, and at some point with soul. Major organs within the body have their chakric correspondence, the chakra being the principle or the cause, the organ being the effect.

4. Also, teachings from three spiritual sources of the world will be used:
    a. the Eight Beatitudes of Jesus the Christ,
    b. the Eightfold Path of the Buddha, and
    c. the Eight Means of Raja Yoga.

With these three we will not only see how various parts of humanity move in accordance with the laws but will see all people can do the same.

The Eight Beatitudes were given by Jesus during His public ministry. Within these simple phrases is the essence of the plight of pain inherent in the human struggle, the duties entrusted to us all as fellow human beings, and the glorious results of living in the heart. The Beatitudes used in this book are quoted from *The Urantia Book*[7]. Their similarity to the gospels of both Matthew and Luke is obvious.

The Eight Beatitudes are:

Happy are the poor in spirit, the humble, for theirs are the treasures of the kingdom of heaven.
Happy are the pure in heart, for they shall see God.
Happy are the meek, for they shall inherit the earth.
Happy are they who mourn, for they shall be comforted.
Happy are they who weep, for they shall receive the spirit of rejoicing.
Happy are the merciful, for they shall obtain mercy.
Happy are the peacemakers, for they shall be called the sons of God.
Happy are they who are persecuted for righteousness sake, for theirs is the kingdom of heaven. Happy are you when men shall revile you and persecute you and shall say all manner of evil against you falsely. Rejoice and be exceedingly glad, for great is your reward in heaven.

---

[7] The Urantia Book, Urantia Foundation, Chicago, 1955. Pg. 1570.

The Eightfold Path given to us by the Buddha is straightforward and succinct. This simple wisdom empowers the individual mentally, enabling one to decide how to live the full range of emotions without their cravings and clingings, leading then to liberation. This enumeration is taken from *Teachings of the Buddha* by Jack Kornfield, with parenthetical additions by DMM[8].

1. Right understanding (of causes)
2. Right thought (thinking)
3. Right speech
4. Right action
5. Right livelihood (living)
6. Right effort (labor)
7. Right mindfulness (vigilance and self-discipline)
8. Right concentration

Raja Yoga is the path of mind and heart blended in the yoga of observation and sustained conscious living. Union (yoga) is sought through understanding the many facets of the self, through the use of mind as a tool of soul, the emotions as soul's reflection, and life as a gift of service to the Soul in All. The Eight Means of Raja Yoga were given to us by the sage Patanjali thousands of years ago. Additional interpretation has been added.

1. Yama - harmlessness, truthfulness, and abstention from avarice, greed, and emotional incontinence.
2. Niyama - internal and external purification, contentment, fiery aspiration, spiritual reading, and devotion to Ishvara (soul, the Word incarnate at any and all levels).
3. Asana - right attitude, position, posture, place and time. Poise.
4. Pranayama- breath, rhythm, life currents, cycles, control of personal forces and energies.

---

[8] *Teachings of the Buddha,* pg. 30. edited by Jack Kornfield. Shambhala Publications, Inc., Boston, 1993.

5. Pratyahara - right withdrawal of the consciousness from the external.
6. Dharana – attention, point of tension; to maintain, sustain, and contain the consciousness where one chooses.
7. Dhyana – meditation; centering the consciousness and thereby the penetration of conscious awareness into the center (medi) of choice.
8. Samadhi – Nirvana, At-one-ment, conscious alignment with the Divine.

As we live the Laws of the Soul we will find that the three paths of Eights increasingly blend becoming an integrated part of the disciple's consciousness. In time, the same will be so for humanity as a whole. For instance, the merciful will use right thought and right action and will therefore be the harmless of yama. The pure in heart will practice right livingness and right discipline and so will move in niyama (contentment) and dharana (attention). As we ponder the laws we will see that the separation of these three lenses will disappear and their coherent functioning in life will be revealed. Then these long lived practices of effort will slip below the threshold of awareness and, like the breath, just be breathed. Therefore, as the last few laws are considered the Beatitudes, the Eightfold Path, and the Means will not be pertinent and so little or no reference will be made to them.

Finally, as a reference point, the greater laws both Systemic and Cosmic will be used. Deity certainly is great, and in His/Her[9] greatness has set laws, immutable and benevolent, by which all life moves, evolves, and returns. The seven laws of the soul are subsidiary to the laws of the solar system, which are subsidiary to the laws of the cosmos. Yet "as above, so below" ever holds true. The small gives insight into the larger and the larger always contains the small. In these correspondences we might see the stretch of consciousness as it descends and ascends.

---

[9] Feminine and masculine pronouns will be used interchangeably throughout this treatise.

The Systemic laws, that is to say, laws that govern the solar system are:	Cosmic Laws, or the laws that govern the cosmos are:
1. The Law of Vibration 2. The Law of Cohesion 3. The Law of Disintegration 4. The Law of Magnetic Control 5. The Law of Fixation 6. The Law of Love 7. The Law of Sacrifice and Death	1. The Law of Synthesis 2. The Law of Attraction 3. The Law of Economy

Figure 1

The seven laws of the soul affect all of life. Soul or consciousness is part of every facet of life, and so as it moves through its many manifestations, we can look for the evidence of its passing. The first four laws have made a dynamic impression upon humanity and each chapter will highlight evidence there for analysis. As we move into the fifth, sixth, and seventh laws we move into more refined designs of soul. Matter is slow in its malleability, but soul is patient and knows that through cyclic impression matter will come to delight in these rarefied designs and will bend to produce the spirit in form for all to recognize. We will find examples of the last three laws and the refinement they convey.

These laws are practical; for if the soul is nothing else, it is a practical entity. To understand matter, to extract from every experience new or renewed knowledge, and to grow increasingly in spirit is the way of soul. Therefore, it is the way of each human being. The difference is that we often forget the basics of practicality. Soul, however, never does.

The seven laws of the soul are given so that we can remember, and live life with increased understanding and a sense of meaning. This interpretation of the laws is offered so that each of us might understand how very close soul is, how relevant these laws are to everyday life, and see the fullness in which one does or does not live. They are given so that we can move with soul's measured pace, as well as its flow. They are given so that we might understand that we are co-creators. We are soul.

Chapter One
Self-Actualization, Initiation, and Hierarchy

Every human being will one day be as illumined and glorified as the Buddha or the Christ. Both Great Ones said so. We are guaranteed illumination or heart-full expansions of consciousness because that is what the denouement of the human kingdom is. Self-actualization is within the grasp of all people because we, of all the kingdoms on this planet, are the only one that has intelligence, love, and will that can be knowingly coordinated and galvanized to a particular goal. Often we employ these qualities in selfishness; but the same three are the only equipment needed to harvest the greatest light, to live in sublime peacefulness, and to empower and thereby free the world. This is no exaggeration. It is a statement known and lived as true by countless human beings through history and living today.

A woman sits in meditation. She had been diagnosed with cancer a couple of years back and with that re-invested herself in her Self. Her mind used to ping around, each ricochet creating a spark of light, an insight, an understanding that seemed revelatory; and although these lighted thoughts were good, her mind was still too active, therefore her life still scattered. One day while in morning meditation with a group that met regularly, stillness enwrapped her like soft cotton. Her mind slowed and watched itself slow, and she meditated truly for the first time. Before this she had been in training, a training that was for one primary purpose: get all the parts of the personality in line with the light and life stream of the soul. Automatically that would mean that the mind would slow down and become sky-like, open, and totally receptive. The emotional self would be infused with love, translucence, and equilibrium. No longer would the emotions dictate the reactions or responses in life. No longer would they determine how she thought or what got triggered. Her emotional body would become a clear cool pond, a deep reservoir of feelings and compassion, of support and understanding. In that moment warm tingles expanded through her chest. They seemed to start at her heart and open up from there, radiating out, touching the world. And light filled her mind. She felt peace, stillness, and bliss.

A couple of friends talk for hours on things of meaning. Life, death, change, holding on. They examine how they move, why they do so in work, at play, with loved ones and with total strangers. One asks if more tea is wanted. They have gone through two pots already, have been talking for hours non-stop, but time was not registering during this soul talk.

Across town, or across national borders, a parent is being told that his son has leukemia. In shock he says, "Oh, my God", and means it. Inside he begins a prayer, an invocation to God to help his son, his wife whom he will have to tell, and to help himself get through this trial of life. "The Lord is my shepherd, I shall not want…"[10] Over and over again he repeats the psalm, just as a Hindu parent would repeat a prayer from the Gita or a Buddhist parent repeat a prayer from the Dhammapadda. The prayer will turn him inward to a place of resolve, strength, and receptivity. It will help him get through this crisis of not knowing and challenged trust.

All of these people have something in common: a relationship to the inner and deeper things in life. They all have a regular job, occasionally get indigestion, angry, frustrated, or sad. Yet, their conscious participation with the inner, to whatever level, is their ticket to self-actualization.

Self-actualization is a process. Therefore, methods to improve or hasten it abound. Those methods are found in various religious practices, meditative techniques, and philosophical understandings. The process is also greatly enhanced through service, or freely giving of oneself.

Self-actualization has many names: illumination, enlightenment, glorification, at-one-ment, union, spiritualization, soul infusion, awakening, becoming, liberation. These are just some of the English words, as the languages of the various traditions around the world have their own words for this process.

---

[10] Psalm 23 from the Jerusalem Bible. See Appendix for full text.

The process of self-actualization is archetypal, and basically the same for all people. That is why the myths, stories, and legends of all who have achieved have common elements. These stories are for our edification; they are the story of how we will do the same. The metaphor of a life is an encapsulation of the way we will achieve Life.

Looking at some of the well-known stories the archetypal journey appears. For example, Christ is not the only son born of a virgin. According to world legends other Sons of God were as well, and these legends predate the Christ story. Mithras, Horus, Zoroaster all are said to be born of unblemished, virgin mothers. Buddha's mother is said to be pure and holy, a sacred vessel that brought forth the light. Whether or not these cases are historically correct is not the point. The symbol of the virgin birth for all these sons of God is that they were the pure soul, born into the world to teach, save, and liberate, and that these lighted beings were born through women who kept their minds and hearts as pure as they could. Furthermore, each person must in some lifetime begin the process of making pure their body, mind, and feelings so that the greatest light can indwell. This is to make virgin ourselves; to take away the stain of materialism; to consciously engage the processes of purification of thought, word, and deed. Thus would a man or woman become virgin. The word virgin is to remind us of two things: our virgin birth as a soul, breathed forth by the spirit of God; and our divine heritage of bliss in the re-union with the God Self that is our higher self, and the ecstasy of that re-union that is incomparable to any pleasure.

Christ was born in a cave stable; Buddha born in a forest as his mother held onto a tree for support. Mithras was born in a cave. This tells us of our common root – in and of the earth. A lowly beginning for kings of the spirit, yet this example reminds us that all of us are the same, regardless of the station we might eventually hold, rise to, or leave behind. Our physical origins are of the earth and our bodies will return back to it. None can escape this. In fact it is the duty of soul to enter into the earth and thereby uplift and change all matter.

Buddha left the castle of his father the king and journeyed into several years of harsh asceticism, living with little to sustain him. Jesus went into the desert for forty days[11] to pray, purify, and to let himself be tested by the dark voices inside. Christ tells the story of the prodigal son who leaves his father's home, wanders in the far off lands, tasting all that there is to be known, but then finds himself destitute, challenged by his inner longings not anymore for material gain but for the solace of love and true companionship. His wanderings brought him to a desert life, empty, barren, and harsh.

Each of these stories tells us that we too must one day, one life time, begin the process of renunciation. That process will leave us with little but our self, its inner strength, and knowing that there is more to life and to living than what feeds the body or gratifies the senses. In fact, as we embark into the desert experience we find that nothing has flavor anymore; that the trappings of life are just that – trappings – keeping us prisoner. Why should we have to give up; why should we leave comfort and that which we seem to know so well? Because to the soul it is only the smallest part of a vast personally unrealized whole called Life. The Buddha left a life of ease to understand why humans suffer, why there is pain and death. Through the rigors of self-imposed asceticism he realized that he was inducing his own pain, causing his own death. He wanted to answer a huge question. His heart's desire, though noble and selfless, was still a desire. Desire held the key to the mystery.

Christ went into the desert because he had just been awakened to the fullness of his self-appointed task in the world, to be a redeemer, a savior. As he was baptized in the River Jordan he heard the voice of his destiny, and the fullness of it down poured into his consciousness. He went into solitude to meditate and pray that he had it right, that he was not personalizing that which was not personal, and to learn to let go the results that would come after he was gone, the results of human intervention and how humanity would take his teachings and use them as well as change them.

---

[11] Forty days is symbolic. 40=4x10. Four is the number associated with the personality, with matter and concretion. Ten is associated with perfection. Jesus was asked three questions, each pertaining to the desire of some part of his personality. He answered righteously in a way commensurate with the spirit seeking to make him perfect. From the spiritual person's and soul's perspective incarnated life can be a desert, dull and barren.

All of us will or have undergone a version of the same experience. Each of us will come to understand that our desire nature is the biggest source of inspiration and motivation, but it is also a ball and chain that shackles us to the wheel of rebirth, over and over again. Each of us has had an insight, revelation, or intuition of responsibility. Yet how many take the time to ponder its implications and the qualities needed within the self to see it through to completion, a completion without ego or desire for recognition or result.

These great teachers lived simple lives among simple people. They lived lives of service to others and to the Godhead. Each of us will do the same. To live simple lives is to be unfettered by want, status, or image. It does not mean that one has to live in poverty, although both these great ones did. It does mean to live free from the stickiness of greed and ego. It is to be a peer to all, respectful and honoring the humanness of each human being. Respect is a rite of passage on the way of self-actualization.

The process itself includes expansions of consciousness that are significant and life changing. It might be only the inner that is changed at first. No one might recognize or be aware of the answered prayer, the dream that was so real, the meditation, or moment that light filled the heart and mind to the point that breath was taken away, time stopped, angels could be heard, or the voice of an inner presence.

I was guiding a group meditation once near Christmas time. As a group we had meditated three times a week for a few months. Yet something had started to happen with each person very quickly. One woman started to feel in a whole new way, a way that allowed forgiveness, patience, and non-judgment to be part of her and how she interacted with others. We had been meditating on compassion for a number of days, and this morning we were completing the process.

Light and love bathed her being. Tears of joy and understanding streamed down her cheeks as she understood why before she could not forgive but now there was nothing more important to do. She was taken over by a breath that breathed grace into her and an allowing presence that washed away whatever hurts she had been carrying. She was embraced by a universal love that she had only heard of before, but never ever could possibly have understood. She was born new in the love of Christ – not religiously, but in the *Christ principle*[12], the principle of Love. She had experienced the first initiation.

There are five initiations for a human being. After that the person is a spirit being; and although there are higher initiations we need not discuss them here. These initiations of consciousness are, again, archetypal. It does not matter if one belongs to an organized religion or not; rank or status within the human experience also do not matter. What is of moment is aspiration, openness, and will. These put us in touch with the good, the true, and the beautiful that is God/dess all around us.

An initiation is a beginning, the process, and a completion. With it we embark upon a new turn of the spiral of life, of qualities grown, and service rendered. It is the result of an inner orientation that probably included some form of spiritual practice – either self made or offered through a philosophy or religion. An initiation is an empowering, a gracing, and often confers a sense of knowing increased responsibility. With an initiation an expansion of consciousness happens that illumines our thoughts, the way we feel, and the way we move that is unmistakable and cannot be denied. This keeps us vigilant to these changes of consciousness and how to implement them in our lives. If we go back to the story of the woman at group meditation, the birth she experienced gave her new eyes to see with, a new found patience and ease with situations that used to be upsetting. Immediately she began to simplify her life, her home, and her relationships. Fears, comforts, and questions militated against significant change before, but now the doors of life seemed open wide, and she, like a child, was eager to experience joy.

Some religions and societies have rites of passage that they call initiations. They are staged and organized events. Kalichakra with the Dalai Lama, as an example, is considered a mass initiation. Thousands of people come to the public ceremony. Many are touched by the profound. Amachi is a Hindu woman saint who travels the world and gives dharsan.[13] Her

---

[12] The Christ principle, the principle of love. It is that which anoints (christos), bringing compassion, light, understanding. It is also called the Buddha nature.

[13] Pronounced darshan. Dharsan is Sanskrit and means "viewing". Dharsan is an opportunity for the public to experience the presence of a saint or mahatma – great soul.

presence is the presence of love and hundreds of people from all backgrounds line up for hours to receive a brief hug from her. Many have experienced grace in her presence. These examples of public events might very well be the setting for a person who is already ripe for an inner experience of consciousness to have or take an initiation, but it will be because he or she is inwardly prepared.[14] The five primary initiations would require a book. This tabulation provides some basic correspondences.

	Symbolic Name	Conditioning Ray	Level	Element
1st	Birth in the Cave of the Heart	7th	Aspirant	Earth
2nd	Baptism in the Waters of Life	6th	Disciple	Water
3rd	Transfiguration or Union	5th	Initiate[15]	Fire
4th	Renunciation, Crucifixion, Liberation	4th	Arhat	Air
5th	Resurrection or Mastership	1st	Master	Ether[16]

Figure 2

Everyone will experience mini initiations between the larger ones listed. The smaller ones are tests of the fullness of life according to where one stands on the Path of Selfhood. There can be large expanses of time between the first initiation and the second, and usually a number of lifetimes between the second and the third. Each of these mini but vital expansions of consciousness *re-key*[17], that is to say heighten the resonance,

---

[14] Alice A. Bailey books on the subject of initiation are: *Bethlehem to Calvary, Initiation Human and Solar,* and *The Rays and the Initiations.*
[15] An individual can be called an initiate from third degree of initiation onward.
[16] Symbolically this means that the master can work freely within five out of seven planes expressing life on this planet.
[17] Re-key – the idea is musical and therefore mathematical. Re-keying is a process of tuning to the note of the soul and staying in resonance with it. The note of the soul is chord-al, thus providing more than one "key" for each part of the personality. Literally,

of the personality to the down flow of the soul. They re-energize and hold in the forefront of the consciousness that which the individual knows inwardly. These events help the wayward son or daughter of God stay on the path of light, and not wander for long into the far off lands of materialism, ego-centricity, or desire.

The first initiation is about the light of love and the development of the mind in ways of wonder, enquiry, and the beginnings of philosophical thinking. The universals of life dawn upon the newly open mind. The fear of death is dealt a blow, and the individual realizes that one is more than just a body and its needs. Likewise is everyone else; therefore equanimity begins to be lived.

The second initiation solidifies the ability to respond, most of the time, in kind with the needs of the moment, emotionally, mentally, and with relative dispassion. The individual has been living the training of emotional reactiveness for lifetimes, and has found it exhausting and painful. The emotional waters, the need to escape (through addictions, isolation, fantasy, etc.), and feeling things viscerally all must be superceded by responsive empathy and compassion. In addition, the second initiation usually propels one into larger areas of service, immediately testing all mentioned above.

The first two initiations are called "initiations of the threshold." They are initiations of the personality into a greater alignment with the soul. They also are planetary, in that they ask the individual to participate in responsible planetary living.

The third initiation brings union between the personality and the soul. The mind, emotions, and physical living are pretty well soul-arized, and although this person still has a personality (and some of the imperfections that go with that) they are primarily a soul. Their consciousness is awake. They understand cause, not just meaning. Their life is one of service as understood by the Law of Service. In fact, at this level of consciousness they live all the laws of the soul.

---

this vibration unlocks the doors of self-knowing, and the key/note/vibration becomes the key unlocking the door of selfhood.

The fourth initiation makes one "a true soul", says the Tibetan master D.K. With this initiation all vestiges of egoity are renounced. In this way, all that is left is the soul-spirit moving through a purified and totally permeated personality. This initiation frees one from the wheel of rebirth and so is also called "liberation." Personal karma is complete and no longer created because one has seen and understood the falsity of personal desires and expression.

The fifth initiation is mastery over five out of seven planes of matter and consciousness. A master is a Great One, a Lord of Compassion, and a Master of the Wisdom.

Hierarchy, or the kingdom of souls, is the workplace of achieved souls. It is an intricate and intimate relationship of soul, spirit, qualities, and energies all being wielded and orchestrated according to the Divine Plan as known in the Heart-Mind of God and understood by the Masters of the Wisdom.

Hierarchy has rank and file as does any large organization. But the unanimity of soul and the overarching purposefulness of the Plan bring peer-ship to bear on all the work and the workers. There is no ego in Hierarchy. One's rank or role are determined by life lived, qualities understood and embodied, and respect for all of life.

Hierarchy has seven main divisions, established according to the Seven Rays. These are called the Major Ashrams. As Gandhi once explained, an ashram is a community created through shared inclinations and work. In Hierarchy the ashrams are communities of souls, incarnate and not, who share work, intentions, and goals. The seven major ashrams are further sub-divided into seven more but these are just further defined aspects of the primary work, according to the ray of the major ashram. As an example, the first ray ashram pertains to the laws of planetary life. This translates into governance understood within each kingdom. For example, within the plant, animal, and human kingdoms the law of supply and demand has different faces and results, yet the law holds true. All large episodes of destruction in any kingdom are assisted by the first ray ashram. Destruction lays waste to old forms and provides opportunity for new forms to be created and developed. These in their turn will one day also be destroyed as the idea embodied or the consciousness indwelling will find the form stagnant and confining.

The laws, esoterically understood, become rules and man-made laws for governance of people, countries, and global life. These, too, are overseen by the first ray ashram. Not all seven sub categories of all seven major ashrams are fully functioning yet. This requires that people who have achieved self-actualization and are conscious souls be able to fill those ranks. Such is not yet the case on all ray lines. This is part of the evolution of consciousness within the human kingdom as a whole. One day souls of all rays will be fully expressing within humanity and within the planet. That day we will, as it was foretold "make of earth a heaven".

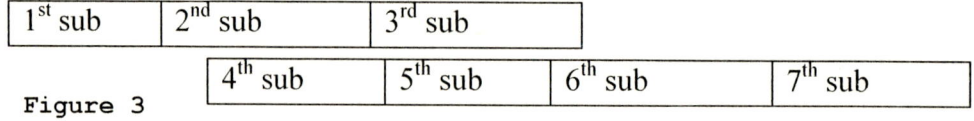

Figure 3

Members of Hierarchy need not necessarily be *occultists or esotericists*[18]. They need not appear holy to everyone. It will be obvious that they have a wider view of the world, and one that is more cause-oriented. They will have detachment and yet a deep empathy.

Through the process of self-actualization and initiations, the mysteries of life unfold to the waking person. Each kingdom holds a mystery to all life, not just that one kingdom. As these mysteries unfold and can be seen as part of the Plan of God, a person becomes a more efficient worker in the world. Again, some basic correspondences:

---

[18] Occultist and esotericist are synonyms. Occult means "that which is hidden," as the sun is occulted during a solar eclipse. That which is esoteric is that which is veiled, hidden, or little known. An occultist or esotericist seeks to know that which is unknown, see that which is unseen, and reveal the mysteries of life.

Name of Kingdom	Expressing Through	Rays	Mystery
Mineral	Concretion	7 and 1	Radiation
Plant	Growth and color	2, 4, and 6	Perfume
Animal	Herd and individual	3 and 6	Finding Source
Human	Unity in Diversity	5 and 4	Intelligence to Intuition
Soul	Light of Consciousness	5 and 2	Alchemy/Redemption

Figure 4

In each case, the kingdom expresses a mystery of life. Each mystery is lived by all kingdoms, but one has the specific purpose of manifesting and perfecting the way in which that mystery can be lived, experienced, seen, and known in the world. For example, all humans become radiatory. It is seen in auras, in the light around sacred people, in the clarity of their thoughts and lives. We depict them with halos or golden disks of light around them. We feel their presence. Thus eventually all humans will achieve the ability to radiate light through their form.

All kingdoms demonstrate perfume, some more obviously than others. Animals have scent and locate each other, their territory, and their food by scent. Humans have scent and in the modern world try to cover their natural body scents with manufactured ones such as soap, shampoo, and deodorant. Certain minerals are easily recognized by their scent. Sulfur, salt, copper are some obvious ones, as well as petroleum.

These examples convey the tip of the iceberg of how the mysteries of Life are in all of life. The same mystery can be recognized and understood as we develop eyes to see, as Christ said. Buddha told his disciples and us to "be a lamp unto yourselves." This means not only to illumine one's own way, but to light the path of knowledge for the world around one through keen observation and spiritual reading of life. As an example, the mystery of life and death is so clearly displayed by the plant kingdom. The constancy and repetition of it season after season, year after year, makes dull our minds to comprehend the freedom that this gentle daily reminder offers. All life is cyclic. Life gives, then gives back to itself so that it can grow anew from the fodder and seeds self sown.

A human being is no different in the fundamentals of life, seeds sown of karma, and the harvest we will gather. Life cycles round. The wheel of rebirth is the turning of the wheel of seasons. Self-actualization awakens us to this fact born out with every seed cast to the wind. We are what we have been. The present moment is created out of the past and will be the seed of the future. We are the lotus flower. We are the sacred heart rose. We are the tree of life growing. The more conscious of that fact we become the more seeds of beauty and empowerment we sow and less seeds of imprisonment, frustration, or greed. The mystery of the plant kingdom is the mystery of the growth of humanity. The mystery of radiation is the key to health, inexhaustible energy resources, and of light. The mystery of scent and finding the source offered through the animal kingdom plays out in plants as they follow the path of the sun. In humans it is our innate directionality first into matter and sought after gratification, and then towards the spirit and a fuller gratification - that of union.

As we proceed to discuss the Laws of the Soul these thoughts of self-actualization, initiation, and Hierarchy are our foundation. The Laws of the Soul are the way in which these processes demonstrate concretely in our lives as individuals and as a whole kingdom. Each of us is at some point in our self-actualization. That point or position on the Path determines how much each of us does or can wield a law and the responsibility that is conferred with that. Life is the measuring stick; we need not judge ourselves or others in this regard. Instead, "by their fruits you shall know them," the Christ said.

Chapter Two
The First Law of the Soul
The Law of Sacrifice
"The Law of Those Who Choose to Die"

The fundamental of this law is the sacrifice of soul. Then what is soul? Who is this being of sacrifice? How can its quiet voice be described, or the subtle sense of belonging it brings be explained? This is not the voice of conscience instilled in us by our parents, cultures, or societies. That voice is much too loud, hasty, and all too often, harsh. The voice of soul is still, small, unassuming, gentle and so powerfully present when it is heard. One questions it because of its simplicity. The mind assumes that which is greater than itself must also be more complex. But as has been said, "the mind is the slayer of the real,"[19] and as such would dismiss the clear power of loving simplicity.

Soul is that which is conscious of its consciousness. In being aware it is aware of far more than itself. Consciousness is an aspect of life and as such that which knows its consciousness shares it with all the rest of life. Barriers of time and space, of appearance and circumstance are transcended by consciousness and therefore by soul. That is not to say that soul is untouched by the constraints of time or that it does not take up space, but there are a few important qualities of soul that render time and space less powerful and less oppressive to soul than to physical man.

Soul has the long view therefore time is not a problem. Soul, being part of the Plan of God, knows that eventually all will work out. This is not the faith of the mystic, this is the knowing of the player who, not only knows his part, but was there when the play was written. Time is only registered as the passing of experience and the gaining of expertise in the various dimensions of matter. Souls knew that temporarily their awareness, power, and even their degree of intelligence would be occulted, obscured, and dimmed by the shroud of matter. Souls knew that they would be blind, deaf, and dumb in a world of results, where causes are not seen, where darkness would be at every hand because the incarnated might not remember its own light.

What is sacrifice? It is to make sacred. Sacred is honoring and respect; it is an attunement to the quality that is real in a person, moment, or event. To make sacred is to move in a way that is without deference, that is to say, without deferring to the form in which the quality finds itself, but instead rejoices with the quality, the essence that the form (of person, place, or thing) is announcing. To make sacred is to move with humility, not bombast. It is to acknowledge every blade of grass, as well as every sadness or gleam of spontaneous joy in the eye of a person. Therefore, sacrifice is to stand ready, willing, and able to allow the processes of the present as we think, emote, heal. It is to give that present quality expression. Sacrifice, then, is a *giving to*.

In Esoteric Psychology, Vol. II by Alice Bailey we read that the Law of Sacrifice is about the "impulse of giving." This impulse is the soul's knowing and understanding of the gift of *giving to*, of giving in-ward, to the sacred essence at hand. A parent sacrifices sleep to the newborn baby in the crib. The parents of teen-agers sacrifice their opinions to the developing self-awareness of growing independence. Trees sacrifice themselves to be wood to build and then heat homes; vegetables in our gardens sacrifice so that we can eat and live. The sacrifice of the soul and this impulse is not begrudging; it has no ego in it. That is because the soul sees and knows the reasons why this or that is done, is necessary, or required.

The impulse of giving is a rendering of more to less, a giving so that there is gain to other, life lived more fully, essentially, easily. It is a precursor to compassion.

The thought of giving, of rendering all, and of sacrifice has long played with people's minds and hearts. It is the reality of our essence seeking recognition. It is the word of the soul as it resounds in the ear of the incarnated person that, yes, people are more than skin and bones; that a

---

[19] I believe this quote is from the Upanishads of ancient India.

person is an incarnated soul, hung pendant between the real and the unreal on the scales of karma and that this is soul's own choosing, knowing. And giving. This is portrayed for us clearly in The Bhagavad Gita when Krishna says "having pervaded the universe with but a fragment of myself, I remain."[20] Krishna exemplifies the soul that will give itself freely into matter and thus reveal the spirit that soul reflects.

In The Bhagavad Gita, Krishna is speaking of an act done before time began. Yet He knew His duty and so pervaded the universe thus giving it soul. In this selfless act not only did He remain whole but the universe could start to perceive its wholeness.

The apostle John tells us the same of the Christ in his gospel. "In the beginning was the Word and the Word was with God; and the Word was God. He was with God in the beginning. Through him all things came to be..."[21] Again before time began a plan was created. Soul was there privy to the intentions of the Divine for all creation. The Plan is that all life will become conscious of the spirit that moves within, that life will know the Life that has pervaded the universe and therefore has pervaded It. To "be" is to become conscious of the soul self, the meaning of one's existence, and the cause of that meaning. This is moving in and with the Christ consciousness, the Krishna self, the Buddha nature. Buddha said, "He who knows the going and returning of beings - the birth and rebirth of life - and in joy has arrived at the end of his journey, and now he is awake and can see - him I call a Brahmin."[22] The Buddha describes a person who has achieved soul consciousness, and therefore, as the soul, "knows the going and returning". This process is the sacred-making of a human being, part of the Plan for all life forms created by a conscious God.

The Law of Sacrifice requires space and time for its functioning. As soul enters into matter a new space is created, a space that is quickened and potentially aware. Soul is the enlivening principle here not spirit. Spirit is still too electric, too powerful to fully enter into the coarseness of

---

[20] *Bhagavad Gita*, translated by Swami Nikilananda, Ramakrishna-Vivekananda Center, New York, 1974.
[21] John 1: 1-3, *The Jerusalem Bible*, Doubleday and Company, 1966.
[22] *Buddhist Texts Through the Ages*, translated and edited by Edward Conzel, Shambhala Publications, Inc. Boston, 1990.

matter. So soul descends, loving both matter and spirit, seeking to bring the two together in a marriage that benefits both.[23]

Deity must descend in order to bring about the ascension of all lives found within the totality. That is the extent of Deity's influence, His radiance, Her magnetism. Descending requires space. It is an entering into. And ascending requires time. Descending is to confine oneself in the thralldom of the matters of everyday life, which is the source of all that is temporary: pain, pleasure, happiness, anger, remorse, excitement, and living. Ascending is to live the processes that lead to liberation. Ascending is to repeatedly break the ties that bind by sacrificing to the greater, more inclusive reality; by acknowledging that the passing moment is passing, is in fact temporary, and that gratification will beget loss, pleasure will produce pain when no longer there. Ascending is to release and rise up Jacob's ladder of light.

Time is another word for experience, and is a key to ascension and liberation. As the consciousness of God sacrifices and enters into the realms of matter all lesser lives are touched. In time they will recognize this fact, register the contact, and be changed; not just by the touch of God, but by their own effort to live in accordance with that which the touch allows life to feel, know, and intuit. Then a new cycle of sacrifice begins, the sacrifice of the little lives, realizing that in giving up what they perceive to be their own they gain so much more.

Sacrifice is to kneel that others may rise. Sacrifice is that surrendering which allows for conquering. In giving up, all gain.[24]

The energy of the Fourth Ray of Harmony Through Conflict, of depths and heights, of compassion so moved as to feel the world, rules this law. The fourth ray is the story of entering into the caves of matter and illusion and from there drawing out life. We lift it up that it might recognize its own light mirrored in the darkness and thereby gain release. This is the

---

[23] Spirit is the source of soul, that which breathed soul forth. Spirit is ultimate, pure, a dynamic center of life. It is one with God-Deity.
[24] *The Labours of Hercules*, pg. 140, Alice A. Bailey. Lucis Publishing Co., New York. 1974.

theme of "I die daily"[25] which the fourth ray knows so well. Knowing the struggles of others and within themselves, so attuned to conflict because of the need to bring about harmony, enmeshed within the multi-facets of life, its expression, its potential beauty, and of the drama of experience itself, the fourth ray literally dies daily, piece by piece, part by part. In steadfastness, and with penetrating persistence, the person with strong fourth ray moves through the waters of the emotions, the fires of the mind, and all the pleasures and pains of the physical existence. Like an empath that does not know how or when to turn off her sensings, pieces of herself are given to others because she feels their struggle, and moves with their movement. This ray wielded by the soul would exude such purity of love that it would empower the conflicted and eventually bring peace.

The Fourth Ray of Harmony Through Conflict And The Ray of Beauty

The harmony of the spheres	is	Synthesis, True Beauty
The ability to work with and in adversity	is	The ability to penetrate to the depths and bring out the light
The divine Mediator, Compromise	is	The divine Intermediary
The Trumpet of the Lord	brings	Enunciation
At-one-ment, unity	results in	Peace
The power to reveal the Path	is	Discernment

Figure 5

The theme of entering into darkness, of descending into Hell (Hades), and of knowing pain and suffering have run through the legends and stories of humankind through the ages. Humanity has always been close to grasping this law. It haunts them, as does their fear of death. Interestingly this fear is but the opposite of the reality that death is something they have freely accepted as souls so long ago as they died to live in matter. Not remembering their entrance into this theater of existence, people suffer. Not

---

[25] St. Paul, 1 Cor. 15:31.

remembering their spiritual heritage, people suffer. Not remembering the fact of oneness that this law attempts to teach, mankind lives and dies separate and unconnected.

But soul remembers. And soul does not suffer as does the emotional or thought bound personality. It does, however, experience differentiation, fragmentation, and a knowing of temporal circumstances. Soul sees itself part and whole at the same time. It feels for the lives it has created and the lives created by Deity Himself. And soul is moved, as is and was God, to uplift and change all existence.

The Law of Sacrifice is the first law because all other laws of the soul are consequences of its enactment. To sacrifice is to Serve. To uplift and salvage is to move in Magnetic Impulse. To recognize the needs of sacrifice is to Repulse. Having done that we become a focal point of change and a point within Group Progress. All life then resonates to these points or seeds of liberation. Expansive Response is the resonance of spirit with spirit. And the Law of the Lower Four gives us the measuring stick for freedom and the assurance of the reality of achievement via struggle and effort.

This law of the soul is akin to the Law of Sacrifice and Death, one of the systemic laws. Death is a value given by the perceiver. In other words, it is the on-looker who has feelings and thoughts about death, not the one who has died. Therefore, our perceptions of death are the result of our longing, fears, doubts, and ignorance of the subjective unseen worlds. In not acknowledging the soul as immortal and as a being of light, death becomes a final fate, horrible to many. But the Law of Sacrifice and Death reveals that all forms must give way to the quality of consciousness within. All presentations of life must have their opportunity to reveal as much of life as possible. Since, however, the form of something always hampers or limits in time-space, the Law decrees that the form which limits must eventually pass away or be destroyed. Plants give us a beautiful simple example of this Law. A seed burst open is no longer a seed; its form is destroyed. The plant begins to grow, changing everyday into something more suited to display the beauty it was designed for. Leaves give way to bud, bud blossoms into flower. The flower is noticed, smelled, and plucked to decorate a table. If left to complete its cycle, the flower will wane, set seed, and die; its death foretold in the original sprouting seed.

Sacrifice and Death, then, become the two sides of one whole continuum; that which the soul calls life the persona calls death and vice versa. Being sense-bounded, the tangible is the measure of the real for the personality. Being released from that limiting measure, the soul understands the cycles of appearance and (apparent) disappearance, of manifestation and destruction. A child is born, and so appears or arrives in the world. A person dies and disappears from the lives of his friends and family. Yet consciousness cannot be destroyed. It can be out of cycle, like a plant dormant in winter. True, the form of the person is not present anymore, nor his talk, laughter, and contribution daily to the everyday world. Yet the gift of consciousness is still there in how we who knew the person were touched and changed through interaction with him or her.[26]

The Law of Sacrifice is also related to the greater cosmic law, the Law of Attraction. It is the desire of Deity to love all and by that love change all in form, in consciousness and in degree of power. God's desire is to express quality through the little lives that comprise Her. And though that quality manifests in various forms, its synthesis is love.

The Law of Attraction is the cosmic law of caring. Attraction pulls at all within the totality of lives and draws them toward the center of life. Sacrifice is knowing that this must be done; furthermore, must be accomplished in order that sacrifice will produce more light, love, and power in all of cosmos. The Law of Attraction states, "Lo, I am with you until the end of the days,"[27] or from the Gita, "I am the goal and the support; the lord and the witness; the abode, the refuge and the friend. I am the origin and the dissolution; the ground, the storehouse, and the imperishable seed."[28]

As we look out to the three worlds we can see how the human kingdom is affected, used by or uses this law. The masses feel the suffering,

---

[26] *Bhagavad Gita*, II: 13. "Even as the embodied Self passes, in this body, through the stages of childhood, youth, and old age, so does it pass into another body."
[27] Matthew 28:20. *Jerusalem Bible*
[28] *Bhagavad Gita*, IX: 18

darkness, and cowardice of the fourth ray. They feel the inertia that fear often causes. Militancy or rebellion against giving is also a very real affect of this law in the kingdom of man.

The Fourth Ray of Harmony through Conflict and the Masses

Conflict lived	struggles with	Harmony longed for
Cowardice	leads to	Feeling embattled
Fear	creates	Inertia
Constant Struggle	fatigues	Result - complacency
Detachment	is part of	Perseverance
Drama	conveys	Pathos
Discernment	brings	Resolution

Figure 6

But the masses are also moved easily by the strong leader, or the gentle voice to change; and change is giving. Detaching from the sense of the singular need, a greater need can be recognized and served. Whole groups of people sacrifice themselves for the betterment of the world. By the actions that this law necessitates multitudes of lives in more kingdoms than just ours are forever changed. Populations of people, like populations of the plant, mineral, or animal kingdoms accept the responsibility of sacrifice and change the thought forms or emotional patterns of the world. Outcries are heard, injustices felt, seen, and known and in response groups of people rally. The loss of life is often great but the liberation of thought and of ancient karma is likewise great. The scales are readjusted. The mind of the World Disciple (humanity) is awakened increasingly to the real. Its emotional (*astral*[29]) patterns are changed, shifted to a higher expression and a greater level of receptivity.

---

[29] astral – usually synonymous with emotional. It therefore is one of the three worlds. The astral world or plane includes all sentiency, psychism, and feelings. For most people, astrality constitutes their first response to life and all circumstances. It is our desire nature as well.

Any great sacrifice can be pondered through this lens of possibility. Manifest Destiny wiped out whole nations of Native Peoples; the plagues in Europe killed hundreds of thousands; Stalin's Bolshevik revolution killed millions. Modern fishing techniques kill loggerhead turtles, dolphins, and other sea creatures knowingly while fishing for other catch. Deforestation and now permafrost thaw are devastating huge tracks of land. In each case, sacrifice and death are the visible rule. Yet the apparent is not the whole and never will be. Karma, dharma, and decisions made by the souls of individuals and groups are rarely seen.

It was said earlier that this law requires space and time. Time takes in the karmic factor. Who will know, except the soul itself, what seeds of karma were sown last existence or thousands of lifetimes ago. Likewise, only the soul knows what dharma, i.e. duty and obligation, it has chosen to take on and complete as part of its contribution to the sacred-making process of the human kingdom and the planet as a whole.

Looking at the Beatitudes, we see that the masses are the "Blessed who hunger and thirst." At first it is the soul that is sacrificed while the personality hungers and thirsts for that which is of form life. We are reminded of the story of the Prodigal Son in the gospels. He left the fullness of his father's home to taste the world. This is the story of the personality. It wanders far and wide through incarnation after incarnation, tasting the fruits of life, living the senses and sensuality of the body, and learning life's lessons. But in time the person finds that regardless of how much one spends, or what material comforts surround one, there is no happiness or peace of mind. Then they begin to hunger and thirst - at first for security, a sense of belonging, and for peace. But all these things still pale by comparison to what the person feels must exist. Each of us recognizes that there is more, and *that* more is spiritual, called by many names, expressed in many ways. It is then that the prodigal thirsts for righteousness.

Righteousness, like other terms used colloquially, loses its meaning. Co-opted by religious sects and dogmas, righteousness for many people is equated with a fundamentalist view of Divinity. This is far from its true meaning and intention. To be righteous is to challenge oneself to stand upright as much as one can, vertical, aligned with the highest Good, in the fullness of Truth, and in recognition of the Beauty of diversity all around. It means to be right with one Self, the Soul self, and therefore with the soul in all. To be righteous is to be pro-active in one's spiritual life, that is, to make it for one self, to take control of one's spiritual growth, and grow. It has little to do with dogmas or doctrines of any one presentation of divine knowledge and revelation. It has to do with one self, and a life lived in accordance with the purpose of that soul-self in the world, i.e. the purpose of an incarnation. Righteousness, then, holds us attentive to the needs of the moment spiritually, giving to the spirit and soul each moment of growth. This is the daily bread spoken of in the Lord's Prayer, "give us this day our daily bread." In other words, the righteous person lives attentive and therefore fed by each moment of each day, and in that can sacrifice in order to make sacred the whole life.

Righteous often has an air of pride or separatism. This is false righteousness; and is based not on the inclusivity of Soul, but on precepts and doctrines. Those who "hunger and thirst" still need to be fed by someone else's thought, beliefs, and rituals. The righteous are learning to feed themselves the bread and water of Life. They have opened the door. Soul will fill their days, their thoughts, and their deeds, once it is allowed entrance. But soul must always wait to be invited. To do otherwise would be against the law of love.

"Theirs is the kingdom of heaven". In other words, theirs is the state of and the understanding of bliss that results from being attentive to each moment, from letting soul and divinity fill their lives through staying aligned, vertical in their spiritual posture, horizontal in their sacrifice, giving to the moment.

Verticality or alignment is both an invocation and its result – evocation. Prayer, meditation, pondering and wondering all put one in a relationship of higher and lower, greater to lesser, abstract to concrete. The vertical of spirit to matter, or of soul to personality creates a channel or corridor of light and life that runs down from source to that which invoked it – the mind, the heart, the person in need. Evocation results. We are evoked, moved in consciousness or understanding. We are impelled to change or implement change in our lives, community, thoughts, or relationships. This creates the horizontal of service, of manifestation and completion. Thus is the cross of life created, vertically and horizontally.

It is amazing how ancient the symbol of the cross is. It pre-dates Christianity by thousands of years. The first settlers of the new world were perplexed to see it used as a symbol in art, clothing, shields, and sacred talismans by the Native peoples. The cross is the relation of the vertical to the horizontal. Esoterically then, it speaks of descent/ascent – vertical, and the horizontal - giving, manifesting, upholding, and supporting. This thought opens the deep meaning of the Christ's statement to "take up the cross". It means to be righteous, aligned, upright, and giving to life. The Law of Sacrifice is just that.

The masses "weep and mourn" not understanding the energies that move them or that for every movement of force or energy there is an equal counteraction. This is the law of karma. Do good and good will be done unto you. Be harmful and harm will come back to you, be it immediately or in some other lifetime. Because we do not understand the basics of sacrifice and economy of energy we suffer. "Why me? poor me" would never be heard again if a person understood that evolution itself is a process of continual sacrifice, of giving to and gaining, but not for the self primarily, instead for the whole of creation.

The Beatitudes tell us that those who "weep and mourn shall be comforted." This is the comfort of soul, of awareness understanding the reasons why things happen. We are comforted because now we can make sense of an event. Soul is trying to teach something, to draw our attention to and illumine something that we just didn't see before. Soul, in compassion and patience has waited and waited, sacrificing itself to the whims of the personality. But soul knows how far to let the string out, and when enough is enough. It is in compassion and divine knowing that the soul then shakes things up, turns things around, and gets our attention. If we could stop long enough and understand, then all self-pity would cease; all sense of separation would end, and life would be seen as the turning wheel that it is.

From the perspective of Raja Yoga we can see that most of humanity does not walk in the harmlessness of yama, not even to themselves. When the reality of soul permeates the thoughts of humanity harmlessness will take on profound dimensions. No longer will the idea be limited to "thou shalt not kill" but will instead take on a positive emphasis. Living in light, in love and understanding and the power that comes with that stance will help humanity walk harmlessly with all forms of life, not just those of its own kingdom. To make sacred according to this law is to choose to die so that others may live. Let us be clear, however, this choice brings greater life to both participants, not less. That which dies is an old pattern of harm. If, for example, an emotionally reactive person could realize that defensiveness in them creates defensiveness or feeling attacked in those around him, that person might choose to change the pattern, understanding now that it does not serve his best interests nor does it make for easy relationships with others. This realization will no doubt be painful at first, realizing that one personalizes, jumps to conclusions, or reacts in a forceful way. But letting this pattern die, sacrificing it to a more responsive way of living, emoting, and relating to others would be a tremendous step toward wholeness and peace.

The Eightfold Path of the Buddha was taught to the masses that they might begin to see the cause of the effects they live daily and that they die for each time they incarnate. It is the un-remembered that is working out in the present moment. If we could understand the continuity of life, that we pick up where we left off, that we are no different than the plant sowing its seed for the coming year, we would take a great step toward enlightenment. The plant grows via the roots that flourished the season before and will stay where it is until it has exhausted the nutrients of experience found within its little plot of earth. We are no different. The Buddha taught that we suffer because of desire; that we incarnate because we have acted in ways that leave business unfinished. We are the plant that continues to sow seed. The seeds that we sow will always grow to fruition. That is the law. The sacrifices we make will, if selflessly motivated, free us from ourselves and free others from us also. We hold on to so many and so much. The law of sacrifice says that we must give to and give up and, in so doing, find that which truly is sustaining.

The Chakras and the Law

There are seven primary chakras in the human energy system. They have location, are related to organs within the physical body, have psychological demonstrations, and are a fundamental tool in our self-actualization. The chakras are the alchemical way-stations within us.

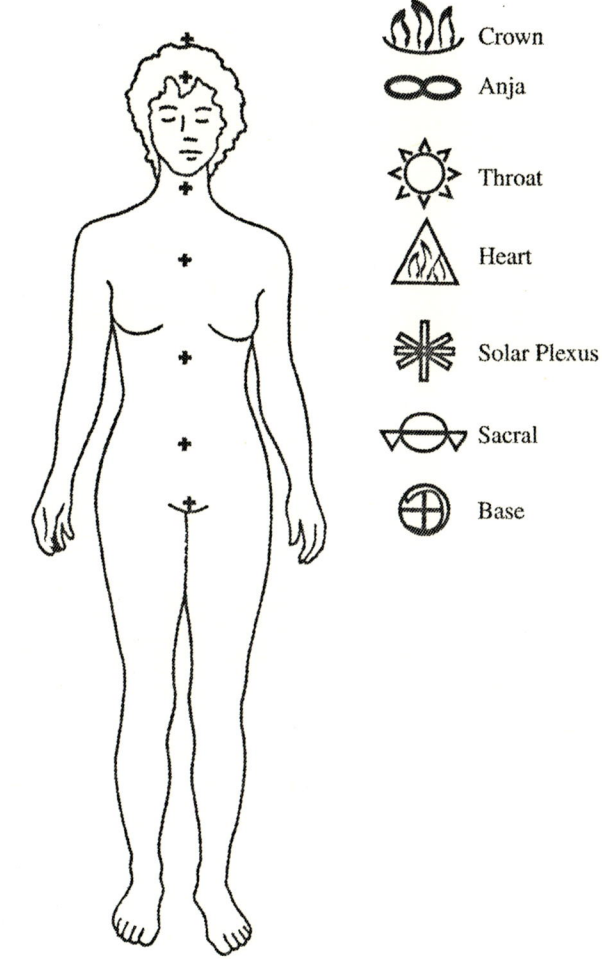

Figure 7

They work with spirit, consciousness, and all types of matter (physical, etheric, astral/emotional, mental, and triadal). The study of the chakras is a science in itself. The wealth of knowledge provided by that study is profound. However, we will touch only briefly on this, using it as just another tool to anchor these laws in our awareness, enabling us to live them more consciously.

Chakra	Soul expression	Personal expression	Tool for Realization	Location
Crown	Will of the Soul	Self will	The blending of intelligence and love into wisdom; love and will into the power to redeem	Top of the head
Ajna	Director of intentions into the world	Coordinates the chakra system	Relates the personality to the soul	Center of the brow
Throat	Creative expression	Expressing the needs of the personality; also thought processes and speech	Eventually is a tool of the mind, providing clarity, prioritization, and relation to concepts.	The hollow of the neck
Heart	The power of Love	Understanding, patience, unattached love	Inclusivity becomes Universal. Serving grows	between the breasts, top center
Solar plexus	Self knowing individual	Personal love, attachment, self reflecting patterns	Non-judgment, respect, allowing	Top of the diaphragm
Sacral	Manifestation, order on the physical plane	Desires and needs, the relationship to the physical plane	Release, moderation, balancing of the yin/yang within	Centered below the naval
Root or Base	Dynamic will in the life; anchoring the will of the soul in daily expression	The will to survive and thrive	will to survive becomes the fiery will to achieve union	The end of the spinal cord

Figure 8

The Law of Sacrifice uses the base and sacral chakras to transmute survival into an awareness of the needs of others. Through the solar plexus and throat an understanding of those needs takes place. Eventually the heart begins to function in love, then all sacrifice, all giving, all saving is made possible. Since the Law of Sacrifice is about descent, it is about the use of the chakras in matter. Again, the soul sacrifices itself into the fullness of matter and loses itself in matter's embrace. The chakras take in these experiences and learn of matter itself, in all its levels and forms. The chakras are the point of intersection of spirit and matter, of intention and creation. But they, like any part of the apparatus of evolving consciousness, become enamored of what pours into them. Eventually that which fed them must be sacrificed for something more refined or of a different type of matter altogether.

As sections of the population undergo a crisis the entire human race is altered. We can see this throughout history. The various empires which have conquered and slain have also brought a different culture to the existent peoples. The religions that have followed each of the Teacher sons of God have blossomed in the yearning, searching psyche of humanity. The teachings were first subject to the law of sacrifice and as such did not remain as pure as the thoughts and truths first embodied but, like souls encased in the flesh, were imprisoned in the limited awareness and vision of the preacher and followers. As groups of people shared in the dispensation of these unfolding truths, the world and consciousness has not been the same.

The giving and use of the mind by groups of scientists or groups of people to a particular medical or scientific endeavor changed the way the world thinks and functions. Therefore, humanity's will-to-be is changed. One example of this was the acknowledgement by the Church and intelligentsia that the earth revolved around the sun. Galileo was not alone in his investigations or findings. He was one of the few, however, that survived the Church's attempt to maintain authority based on doctrine and ignorance. The Inquisition and claims of heresy could not refute or derail the scientific discoveries of the time. His recant to the Inquisitors did not invalidate his astronomical findings through the telescope. The evidence was irrefutable and corroborated by Johannes Kepler in Austria. This rocked the authority of the Church. Nature and the scientific enquiry of nature dethroned the infallible authority of the Church and helped to initiate the separation of mind from belief, of superstition from reason, and of church from state.

Another example is Columbus' excursion across the Atlantic Ocean. He certainly was not the first explorer, nor the first caucasian to reach the shores of the American continents, however, the wave which he rode was the wave of pioneering. Although he did not intend to be an explorer, he inaugurated a cycle of exploration that humanity is still experiencing. His journey across the Atlantic opened the world to the Europeans, who then explored and mapped it, cataloged and colonized it. They also plundered it decimating native populations and exploration became the right to claim and own by the sheer fact of power. The point is that humanity is still exploring. Since Columbus sailed the ocean blue, exploration of rain forests, mountain ranges, oceans in their fullness, Antarctica, and space proceeds with energy, effort, and a methodical approach. Scientific discoveries and globalism made possible a growth in collectivism that was not part of the human consciousness before this cycle began. We live with those discoveries daily, and globalism is the birth point of Peace Corp, the United Nations, NATO, and the Red Cross to name a few.

Global warming directly streams out of the above example. Human interaction with the planet is a major contributing factor to global warming. Scientific evidence suggests that the planet goes through its own cycles of warming and cooling as a natural part of the planetary ecosystem, however, the affect of human consumption, pollution, deforestation, and oceanic depletion all contribute to global warming. The population as a whole is made aware and must make choices, must sacrifice for the sake of the greater whole.

Divine will is anchored in the consciousness of the human kingdom as a result of this type of scientific mind expansion through gained knowledge and work. Looking at other examples, not necessarily related to science but to global living and sacrifice/giving to, we see drought stricken parts of Africa where we are faced with the choice of helping and brotherhood or selfish denial, the United Nations where countries give up just a little sovereignty to work as a new group for the betterment of man. Other examples are Greenpeace, The Peace Corps, Physicians without Borders. Locally we find teachers' aides, mentors, volunteer groups in general, not to mention the plant, mineral and animal kingdoms and their supreme sacrifices daily. All of these are of the masses, whether it be human masses or of another kingdom.

The disciples of the world work with an increased knowing of this law. They have reached up or within and have been touched by soul, therefore have begun to recognize the reality of being more than mere flesh and bones and of life being more than a crap-shoot or the joke of a God with a weird sense of humor. A disciple walks with ever greater compassion and a discriminating mind, and so is increasingly aware of the needs of soul (deity), man, and the lesser kingdoms.

The Fourth Ray of Harmony through Conflict and Disciples

Steadfastness, endurance	leading to	Equipoise
Ability to discern the light	leads to	Equilibrium
Compassion	is born of	Empathy
Decisive assessment	brings	Forward movement
Fearlessness	leads to	Fighting for justice
Harmonizing, Compromising	leads to	Wholistic Relating
Perspective	brings	Relativity
Pairs of Opposites/ Dichotomy	leads to	Synthesis, Resolution

Figure 9

Here the fourth ray demonstrates as steadfastness, endurance, compassion, and the ability to see through the darkness to the light. Empathy and assessment happen, of all sides of an issue or situation, because then the disciple can, to the best of his ability, give what is needed in the moment.

Here again we have space and time, space being the situation, the circumstance, the need, and time being the moment of that need or event. But the disciple is not always correct and so like all other human beings still learns through suffering, both of those he has tried to help and his own; this being the lived experience of good intentions and not always good results.

The use of the solar plexus puts the disciple en rapport with all lives. The heart teaches him what true giving is. The throat helps him adapt to the need of the given situation and to discriminate that which he can truly give. Ajna helps him see where he has been, what he has done and to see the affects of his actions. He begins to see the results of his use of the law and its use of him. Here the personality faces its dweller (the shadow side, the less refined or unredeemed parts of the self) and must decide its degree of sacrifice, seeing the worth of all forms of life.

The disciple is still somewhat attached to the form and so endures fear, cowardice, and inertia. This same disciple has begun to understand the cyclic movement of energies and is not so moved by forces anymore. He is learning to stand still as the tides of time and events move around him. He has learned a degree of harmlessness and asana (right attitude, right position). He now has an understanding, though limited, of the pranayama (breath) of Deity. He begins to hold himself at attention (dharana) that he may see the right action to be taken, hear the right word to be spoken, know the right thought. "Blessed is the pure in heart" and "the persecuted" striving to see God. He is gaining that wonderful fourth ray quality of perspective, a hard won effect of the Law of Sacrifice. It is perspective that moved Deity to incarnate, wanting to give greater perspective to all lives.

Perspective is gained by the masses as whole ideas have been grasped due to the sacrifice of the many. Perspective of soul, perspective of God, of himself, the disciple, in relation to all other lives is now in his growing awareness. He, like the soul so long ago, cannot turn back but can only go forward, deeper into the darkness of the matters of his brothers and sisters and from there draw the shadows out into light. This requires an aspect of the first ray that is found in the fourth ray. It is a fearlessness used in battle, in courage, in compassion, and in the pure empathy of knowing your fellow human beings. It is this that will lead the disciple into greater depths and hence into greater service which in turn will translate into the passing through the doors of illumination and initiation (another great cyclic sacrifice) and entrance into the Hierarchy of the Workers of Light.

Initiates use this law. The masses have been affected and the disciples have been used by it, but initiates know the energies they wield. They understand the limits of space and the pulsations of time. They stand crucified in matter, aligned vertically to Divinity's heart and horizontally to all fields of service. They move through opposites knowing synthesis. They live perspective. In compassion, empathic, but detached from the form, the initiates can work in conflict knowing harmony. Initiates see the beauty hidden by the encasements of lives. They know the giving required and the giving already done. They are the Beautiful Militants, the Warriors of Harmony, the Givers.

The Fourth Ray of Harmony through Conflict and Initiates

Intuition	leads to	Direct Action
Paradox	resolves to	At-one-ment, Essence
Beauty Seen and Acknowledged	leads to	Revelation and realization in the world
Sacrifice	leads to	Redemption
Dispassion	is born of	Mercy (and vice versa)

Figure 10

Sacrifice is a vital part of their consciousness, but greater is the intuited knowledge of the sacrifice of each and every life, cell, planet, and plant. They can do nothing except continue to give and thereby save, for this is the law of the saving forces and the redeemers.

The purpose of sacrifice is to redeem, to uplift, and to change. Evolution spins out of this law. Spiral activity is its motion as is the swinging of the pendulum. The initiate has learned correct action and reciprocal movement and so to the world he stands still - the center of the balance and not the floating scales. Heart, base, and head chakras are employed in loving compassionate action, surrender of the self, and in dedication to the

Source. They are the "meek" and the "peacemakers" of the Beatitudes in the midst of the harmonizing conflict. The law has become an exercise in the use of the fourth ray, at-one-ment and purposeful compassionate action, done through love, leading the world to harmony. They are the Eightfold Path. They walk in Yoga (union).

The Law of Sacrifice is voluntary to the soul. Soul in knowing this took it upon itself, eons ago, to enter into the confines of matter. In doing so the prison eventually is rebuilt into the temple.

Sacrifice is an act of will, the will aligned with the genesis of will - God, the Source of All. As such sacrifice is not a negative but instead a most positive act, done in free will, the will of soul that knows the will of God. The Christ said, "I know the Father and the Father knows me." Christ is the soul made flesh, and the soul is the Christ there in the beginning with God. As such the soul knows the plans of God, and of course chooses to be part of those plans. There is nothing else in the long run. Being aware, the soul chooses to be economical and not waste time or energy. Thus does the soul enter into the latent gold of matter, and begins to build not an altar for sacrifice but a temple of consciousness.

Chapter Three
The Second Law of the Soul
The Law of Magnetic Impulse
"The Law of Polar Union"

A whirling dynamic spiral spins in a revolution that cannot be stopped. It beckons all within its radiance to enter and become part of its momentum. It harkens of wholeness and unity, of integrated coherent work done in unison and selflessness. Its vibrations are varied yet pulse to one vital rhythm. All are drawn into its movement. All are swayed its way. All become part of the ever increasing hum and sound which are its life and its echo through space. None are left out or behind. The knowing participate, like instruments in a great orchestra. The less aware are brought along and become part of the percussion section or a harp string to be plucked, unknowing yet so integral.

This spiral revolves upward, reversed from the spiral that impelled all to enter into the dark fertility of matter. Like a tornado, it lifts all up making them part of its center, its revolution, its essence. And with the entrance of each being the turning becomes stronger, more attractive and magnetic. None can escape its pull. None want to.

Upward, upward, round and round all lives are lost in relationships, in networks of spinning light. The sense of I and mine blend. All direction is lost in one direction, seemingly not one's own, but of a greater force, a collective force, this dynamic spiral.

Upward, upward, round and round. Friction becomes magnetic interplay; a vital free flow of interactive energies. Singularity becomes lost in one - one mind, one heart, one work, one act. One.

Upward, upward, round and round.

Upward, upward, round and round.

Until... the top of the spiral is sensed by souls, no longer single but inextricably woven and bound by love and all that love is. Their singularity is no longer a part of their moved consciousness. The spiral opens out, like a black hole, to a vastness so complete it is All. Like a tornado, the top opens to the endlessness of the blue sky where all life resides, hovering, vital, electric. The top of the spiral is breath itself and all swept into its vortex of metamorphosis have been part of a great breathing exercise, an excellent pranayama.

Then like the breath, the end becomes the beginning of another cycle. All that were swept into this dynamic loving embrace spiral down again into the fertility of matter. But oneness is their movement, love is the spiral in which they walk drawing all unto them, for they see no separation, no I and mine, you and thine. Their power is in the use of all lives and the potential offered by all. Their minds are en rapport.

New spirals walk and turn; upward, upward, round and round, and all lives are drawn into them. They cannot resist. Nor do they want to. They hear the hum of themselves as their soul sings and plays its part in this great cantata, this symphonic resolve, this united glory.

Soul is the great relater, relating spirit to matter, light to darkness, real to the unreal.

It is the organizer of all relations among kingdoms, among the parts of the personal self, and groups within humanity as well as all other kingdoms.

In order to be the relater and organizer, soul's interest is primarily quality. Soul must know the qualities of energy, of *vehicles*[30], and how those qualities may or may not work together.

Soul's interest in forms is that they are the manner in and through which qualities appear in the worlds. Soul sees the greater picture, because it is not mentally or emotionally limited by attachment to form. As such, soul understands the meanings of things, events, and cycles, and is undeterred by the temporary set-backs seen only within the three worlds.

---

[30] Vehicles – our mental, emotional, physical, and etheric or auric bodies. The self (personal or the soul) is the driver of each of these vehicles or parts.

The three worlds of human endeavor are the first place where the human soul learns about quality. The world of the mind is one of mentation, analysis, and discrimination having the quality of dissection, of taking something apart before it can put it together. This process of parts has long lead each soul deeper into ways of form and form management, as well as identification with that which is seen, touched, and can be categorized. The world of the mind eventually leads to unification, putting the parts back together into a better functioning whole. This includes concepts that convey large philosophical truths or render the metaphysical into conversant postulates. This world is often associated with the element fire. In astrology it is associated with air.

The world of emotions, associated with water, includes not just feelings and the full range of emotions, but much of our creative imagination, longings, aspirations, and loves. It is because of humanity's anchor in the emotions that we react, personalize, need, desire, and eventually aspire to more than whatever is the current status quo, as an individual and as a collective. The limited emotional range of anger, jealousy, attached love, and desire for things or comfort grow slowly into an allowing presence and Love – unattached to person or outcome. Also grown is the freedom from having things as a measure of selfhood.

The physical world is all that we see, smell, touch, taste, hear. It is also what we move in and through – living, breathing, dying, and coming back again. The etheric part of the physical world is the health aura of people and plants, the chakra system, and the electrical currents that are part of the manifestation of the planet, so that it can be said that "we live and move in a sea of energies". To the scientist, the etheric would include the ultra and infra wavelengths of light, all forms of measurable radiation such as gamma, and x-rays, radio signals, and the magnetosphere. The etheric level of matter is measurable and quantitative, but usually not seen by the naked eye. The element associated with the physical plane is earth or desert.

These three worlds are what human beings move and grow in. Obviously, the three lower kingdoms, mineral, plant, and animal, do as well. In these three levels of matter humanity feels comfortable and makes its way.

The human soul grows to understand that these matters are not all that is. Furthermore, the soul learns that full ranges of quality, beauty, and essential meaning are contained or trying to be revealed through the forms and masks found in the three worlds. The more conscious a person is the more they see. Psychology is one way that mass consciousness is being opened, seeing what is under the expression of the individual. Art is another. Some people revel in the quietude and beauty of a forest. Others see cleared land and dollar signs. A friend of mine walks a beach on Cape Ann, Massachusetts everyday. Living in Rockport, she invites the rhythm of the waves, the rising sun, and etheric life pulse into her being. Her face is always golden, like the sun on the water. She is aware of the calm and quietude that this repast gives her, how it feeds her emotionally, mentally, physically, and spiritually. Many other people, even living in the same town, don't have that appreciation or relation with the quality found within the three worlds. Because she does it makes her very good at her profession as a multi-cultural trainer. She easily tunes into the quality differences of one culture from another. She then can teach those cultural, ideological, social, and philosophical distinctions to immigrants and business people. She is excellent at what she does because she works with the qualities and not just the forms that those qualities appear through.

Magnetic Impulse. What is meant when we call something "magnetic?" It is usually dynamic. We sense a movement within it or ourselves as are we are pulled toward its centering force. It is unalterable. Iron filings have no choice but to be moved or stood on end as the magnet passes over them. The North Pole affects migrating birds, electrical equipment, and key chain compasses. We count on it for navigation and orientation. Likewise, we are attracted to a magnetic person. It could be sexually or charismatically, but we are drawn into their aura or influence, even if only temporarily.

The other word contained within the name of this law is "impulse." Impulse is forward moving, non-static, and far from inert. It is driven by an inward beat (im-pulse). Impulse requires action but often our action is the result of not thinking and just going along with the mood of the moment or the prevailing influences around us.

The Law of Magnetic Impulse uses attraction within the plane of mind (where soul resides) and is concerned with the results set in motion by that use. Unlike the Law of Sacrifice that allows the individual to give herself to the greater good of the whole and thereby become whole, the Law of Magnetic Impulse begins with the group and with its dynamic interrelations. It starts with a magnetic, attractive draw on all that lies within the reach of a vibration. Soul, the heavenly knower of qualities, builds a meticulous network of living light, magnetically connecting the right polarities in union so that each connection in this vast geometrical pattern will remain firm and secure.

Magnetic Impulse is divine geometry, a beautiful array of light coordinated by intrinsic essential quality. Designs of thought and concept are formed through the attunement of quality, pole to pole, point to point and create something that was not there before, but was part of the Grand Design of Consciousness. An example is the World Ecumenical Council. Leaders of religions from all over the world gather together, not to discuss the differences in their doctrines, but to unveil the underlying similarities in their beliefs and practices. Religion, one of the major causes of war and discrimination throughout history, becomes a mural of the revelation of God and God's heart-mind to humanity throughout time. No one religion is right or wrong. All are part of the out breath of Deity's love for all His creation.

The Second Ray of Love Wisdom

Universal Love	Leads to	Wisdom and a wise understanding of life
Upholding and support	Reveal	Light, and the light in life
Preservation	Is	Withstanding, and standing with
Attraction and the quality of magnetism	Works with	Relating through essential quality

The saving force	Are those who live	Compassion and divine dispassion
Inclusivity and expansion	Brings	Illumination
The Word Incarnate	Is	The principle of consciousness wherever it is found.

Figure 11

The Second Ray conditions this law of the soul. The second ray reveals, through love and wisdom, the divine intention of God. All religions of the world, organized and politicized, tribal or pagan, have certain things in common: love as a feeling of union with that which is greater than man; being mentored or taught by a representative of deity or by deity him/herself; the presentation of divine wisdom in our surroundings and circumstances, hence oracles, superstitions, prophecy, and the search for meaning of the average person; the idea of an intercessor between the individual (be that a person, a nation/tribe, or the world) and the Creator/Creatrix; and the idea of salvation, illumination, and satiety begotten through a relationship with the divine, either transcendent or immanent. All these are the gifts of the Second Ray energy moving through humanity and working with the collective consciousness.

A few examples of each of the above are:

Love and union with the greater – our primal relationship to the sun, the pleasure and peace that we receive from it; mysticism and the mystical experience as it runs throughout all spiritual and religious practices; devotees of Kali, Krishna, Isis to name but a few; brides and handmaids of Christ.

Mentoring – Odysseus by Athena; Moses by Yahweh; Arjuna by Krishna; the apostles by Christ.

Divine Wisdom in our environment – spirit qualities in animals as taught and understood by the Native people around the world.

Intercessor – Isis as a mother and widow, and as the power behind Pharaoh's throne; the Greek or Roman gods, to ask one god to help with a situation akin to their particular power or expertise; Mary or the saints.

Salvation – Isis, Mithras, Ahura Mazda, Jesus

Illumination – vision quest; asceticism or austerities as a means to this end; meditation and mindfulness from any practice; nirvana or samadhi.

The Second Ray is the ray of universality. It is easily seen how universe-all the message of quality is throughout time and through all cultures. Uni – one, verse – sound, all – one word cycling through the ages. One word is the note sounding through all religions, mystical experiences, and even scientific enquiry. That word is Love – and the wisdom required to live accordingly. Illumination, salvation, the use or need of intercessor, the teachings and the teachers, as well as our relationship with the love of the Divine all are Second Ray expressions and are the working out of the Law of Magnetic Impulse.

Magnetic Impulse is the out-picturing of quality to quality, light to light, affecting, uplifting, and fundamentally changing that light or quality into something more refined, which then affects and uplifts more in turn. The Second Ray is all inclusive. It is about the whole and all contained within that whole. As such it leaves nothing out or unchanged. The Second Ray is also about complete wholeness for a human being. Therefore, this ray and this law move a person automatically closer to that eventual glory and liberation.

Humanity's masses feel swept, moved by a current larger than life. They are not sure what is happening but they don't want to miss out. Inclusiveness is the origin of this human trait; to be included, to feel left out of something, or to feel that it is important to participate with something that others are doing all stream out of the quality of inclusion. A person's comprehension of a situation can be enlarged by greater thought and involvement as friends, family members, or co-workers get involved in hobbies, literature, political questions, or enquiry of any kind. An example is the global environment. Slowly through the work and effort of organizations such as The National Geographic Society, Greenpeace, The Sierra Club, The Green Party, and The Audubon Society the masses have been swept into a recognition of the interrelatedness, and the multi-levels of the life systems of our planet. Slowly through magazines, television programs, and wildlife sanctuaries the message of these organizations has seeped into the mass consciousness and has swept it onward and upward to the point where our children remind us of our wastefulness.

The masses feel friction at first, as they are put in contact with ideas not their own or what they are used to. Again the environmental situation proves a good example. How long did it take the thought of recycling to become a more accepted avenue of waste management than the usual "throw away" mentality? And due to the growing piles of recycled materials manufacturers were forced to make good use of these readily available resources. It is the insistent voice of the people that calls for change, a change they could not envision even twenty years ago. Reorientation is taking place.

People also respond as their normal living patterns are altered by the weather changes the world is currently experiencing. They tell stories to their children of when "we had real springs and summers, and when the snow was always deep." They attribute the weather changes to abuse and misuse of the earth's resources and, due to their discomfort or dislike, are moved to change their habits of consumption and to become more educated in areas of resources, recycling, and co-habital living. But the way in which most of this happens is so subtle. Drawn in by curiosity, new trendy ways of living, or by the sense of real need, people begin to act and think in a more wholesome manner. As a result all humanity is changed, uplifted in consciousness and in action. As a result of this our relationships with the lesser kingdoms are changed and thereby our livingness with the planet. Little by little the masses are moved more in line with the divine will of Deity, swept into Her all encompassing love for all lives within Her Great Life. Upward, upward, round and round.

Of the Buddha's Eightfold Path, we can see right action and right behavior starting to be established. Also some right thought is starting but many of the masses just follow along, doing what they are told. They sense the rightness of the idea but do not necessarily understand all the reasoning.

Harmlessness is seeping into the consciousness of the many. Little by little the definition of harmlessness is expanded to include the other kingdoms, such as in the case of animal testing or the way in which animals are penned and force fed only to end up on our dinner table. The thought of harmlessness includes pollutants and contaminants put into rivers, lakes, and oceans, or dumped into landfills and the affects of those actions, short and long term on people, the environment, and the animal populations, not to mention its affect in general water, ground, or air pollution. These examples show clearly that this law of the soul is about the wholeness of the systems of life, each part being made more aware of the other parts, and the symbiotic relations that have always existed and always will.

Harmlessness is foundational to living in concert with life. It is the first means to Yoga, and probably the most comprehensive. As a member of humanity learns to be more harmless to him or herself and to others that affects many people, changes many habits, and makes one ever more thoughtful on a regular basis. Again the wholism of this law illumines itself.

Following on these two thoughts, a Beatitude seems relevant. "Happy are the meek, for they shall inherit the earth." The meek frequently are drawn in. Their innate harmlessness and want of right behavior seem to attract them toward a greater center often unwittingly. They are swept into a force of which they become a part, and they feed it as it feeds them. The earth they will inherit will be a changed existence, as they have been changed and all of life has been changed, reoriented, revolved, reinterpreted.

The Second Ray of Love Wisdom and the Masses

Conditioned and attached love	Leads to	Wanting to be loved Needing to be needed
The sense of belonging	Leads to	Sacrifice without full thought
Wanting to help	Becomes	Comfort zones that make one inert
Fear	Leads to	Timidity, shyness; being reserved
Sensitivity	Births	Nurturing, parenting, teaching
Caring	Leads to	The ability to receive
Giving	Develops	from others, mentally, emotionally, physically

Figure 12

    Each of the Rays contains gifts given by the brother and sister rays. This idea is captured well in the old fairy tale of Sleeping Beauty where each of several fairies blessed the newborn baby with a gift. It is said that the Rays do similar at the beginning of great cycles of planetary development. These aphorisms, so they are called, are rendered in beautiful poetic verse in *Esoteric Psychology Vol. I* by Alice Bailey. Like the expert blending of color to highlight a nuance in a painting, the Rays elicit and enhance certain qualities within the other Rays. This provides the spectrum of qualities within each Ray.

    The Third Ray spoke to the Second Ray, "Draw to thyself the object of thy search. Pull forth into the light of day from out the night of time the one thou lovest."[31] The qualities here are attraction, friction, and time. Some do not know the benevolence of this magnetic pull and they drag their feet. The friction of dragging rounds out the sharp edges of qualities still coarse and unredeemed, and rounds out the contours hard to place within the geometric design of any given intention. Even when pulled

---

[31] *Esoteric Psychology, Vol. I*, p. 66.

willingly, friction results, like the drag on the wings of a plane or of a bird in flight. There again, it becomes a honing process whereby even the good becomes better. "From out of the night of time" and "into the light of day" (the center and top of the spiral) the cosmic lover draws the ones He lovest.

At this level of movement within the Law of Magnetic Impulse the solar plexus is engaged bringing with it a positive feeling or a familiarity. Commonality and the psychic unity of life are felt through this chakra. Its motion resembles the action of this law. Spiraling round and round, it moves all forces of the lower three chakras (base, sacral, and itself) upward to the higher transmutative centers (chakras). There the energies are again reoriented and sent not only down to redeem and reorient the matter of the lower self but to other beings and the centers within them. Much friction takes place; hence the heat of this center.

Within the realms of mass consciousness is curiosity, generally a fifth ray quality. Again using the environmental example, people are investigating their choices as to what to buy, how it's packaged, and how to use their refuse. Reading labels is the norm for many. This leads to education and a greater knowledge of the world around one, as well as the responsibility that each member of humanity has to the rest of the world. Curiosity "leads the sons of men from off the path of knowledge on to the path of understanding."[32]

The masses have been used by the Law of Magnetic Impulse and as so have been pushed or impulsed forward drawing a multitude of lesser lives along with them. Disciples, as should be expected, sense this law, but might not know or understand its extent. Of course this is dependent upon the clarity of contact of that disciple with soul. This is the law of relationships, magnetic, attractive, and interactive. The degree of established soul contact within the consciousness of the tireless disciple will determine his ability to use this law and follow its precepts. Otherwise he is little more than his brother of the masses. Awake though he may be, he also dreams, and in dreaming is swept into the great vortex of the Will of God. The connected disciple, however, recognizes others as soul and endeavors to

---

[32] Ibid.

work, as does the Second Ray, with the contacted qualities abundant within each member of Life. Dynamic and alive are all interactions. Cognizant of forces, increasingly understanding energies, the soul-infused disciple will work with all, according to the greatest measure of the relating-other's abilities. This is key. The disciple and worker with the law must work within the framework of the co-workers abilities, else the intention cannot manifest. The chain is only as strong as its weakest link.

The Law of Magnetic Impulse is about the accurate discernment and use of quality. The raison d'etre of this law of the soul is to identify the possible areas of consciousness that can be used and lifted up to a greater and more elevated application. Being a law of the soul, and since soul is omniscient in space and in time, she can see to the very depth and meaningfulness of all that stands before her. The real is revealed in the now, alluding always to the past and a portent of the future. Quality unmasked and radiant is now available to be called upon, soul to soul, and to be blended and fused through interaction and coherence. Points of light connect and are held together by polarity. Discernment reduces all energies to the most essential point of positive and negative, emitting and receiving. The right use of this wisdom creates the colors and sounds of distinct characteristics, varying levels of consciousness, and reactions that are new creations in and of themselves.

So interactive and networked are these qualities that only the full consciousness of soul could maintain the understanding and scope of their meticulous entirety. Were we to ponder on such as this the extent and tremendous over-arching completeness of the Hierarchy would stand before our eyes.

Hierarchy is the kingdom of souls. It is comprised of all who have achieved a level of consciousness that has tipped the scales of everyday thought and action into soul-full, lighted wisdom regardless of particular religion, philosophy, or profession. Hierarchy is known by many names through history: the communion of saints, the Great White Lodge or Great White Brotherhood (having nothing to do with race, but with the radiance of their light), the Assemblage of Light, the Adepts, The Saving Force.

Hierarchy is a pyramid of Love, Intelligence, and Power comprised of human beings, with those of the highest spiritual achievement at the apex, such as Buddha and the Christ. Others in the top echelons might be the souls who were Moses, Lao Tsu, Ramakrishna, or Plato. The spiritual term "master" means someone who has perfected themselves and their knowledge. Masters have freed themselves from the confines of the three worlds but seek still to serve within them. Their radiance, compassion, wisdom, and skill in action are superhuman compared to a normal person. Their work is the work of goodness, enlightenment and empowerment in all departments of humanity. Some of these great souls (mahatmas – like Mahatma Gandhi) also work with the lives within the other kingdoms.

Hierarchy is built on and out of the workings of the Law of Magnetic Impulse. The fullness of it, its intentions, projects, and the wondrous ability to blend qualities synchronistically is mind-expanding. Our breath would be temporarily taken away by the multi-leveled, multi-dimensional, inter-planetary, instantaneousness of the wise use of quality. Ashrams are built upon it. Kingdoms evolve through it. Planetary purposes manifest as a result of the use of this law. Upward, upward, round and round all are drawn into the waiting loving embrace of Soul and souls.

Disciples come to know their fellow workers by the qualities known and sensed. Masters observe their would-be chelas (students) from afar over long periods of time, watching qualities wax and wane and eventually become steady. Then the experimentation takes place. Qualities in various people are put in contact with one another as events in life put us in relationship with our fellow brothers and sisters. Tension and contact, interactive processes, and earnest effort often unconscious, hopefully produce something that was not existent before between these people in their corner of the world. Groups of quality form; and subsequently may use quality. Consciousness in the participants expands to include their brother's and sister's consciousness. Work can be done that is of a quality much higher than any dreamed being performed by one person alone. More than reorientation this is externalization - to make manifest the intentions of the Divine Plan. The Hierarchy and all its ranks began this way and will continue to evolve this way for this law is its law. Externalization can and will take place as it is already doing because this law dictates it to be so.

"Happy are the pure in heart, for they shall see God." This beatitude tells us that the God revealed to the disciple is the God of qualities seen in each person and each moment, these to be used in harmony and in joy. As a result all qualities are drawn up and rarified. For example, as trust is used and demonstrated by fully awakened disciples it pulls at the innate trust in the masses. It beckons to the many to be more trustworthy and to accept that responsibility that demands that we act and live in a trusting way so that others will not be deceived or lied to in thought, word, or deed. The spiral draws right action into it and multiplies it.

The Second Ray of Love/ Wisdom and Disciples

Response-ability	Bears	Thoughtful action
Understanding	Leads to	Awareness of meaning
Calmness	Births	Non-reactiveness
Brotherhood/Sisterhood	Leads to	Egalitarianism
Detached Love	Leads to	Platonic love
Receptivity	Develops	Sensitive to vibrational impressions from others
Wide caring	Leads to	Support
Stoicism	Leads to	Mental pride
Need for emotional or personal insulation	Becomes	Aloofness

Figure 13

All of the Buddha's Eightfold Path pours forth as disciples work in unison. Right understanding of essence and of some small part of the designed plan help the grouped disciples to hold their minds steady in the light of the soul, where thought and thinking processes become part of the bringing of light into the collective consciousness of humanity. This increases the awareness of right speech and right action on a large scale. Right living, labor, self-discipline, and concentration all result from the first two of right understanding and right thinking. If we understand our options, and understand that everything that one does affects so many others, then that person will make better choices of livelihood. At this stage in humanity most people don't have or don't know of options. As the laws of the soul continue to work with individuals and with the human kingdom as a whole, that will change.

The Eight Means of Raja Yoga become the way of life. Knowing the Sanskrit terminology or not, the disciple embarks on the path of conscious union with the soul in herself and in all. *Yama* is lived. Harmlessness, truthfulness and abstinence from all the pulls of greed, avarice, and turbulent emotional waters are established in the interplays of life. The disciple is reconciled with Self and the Self in all and as such moves in *Nijama*. External and internal purification becomes the process by which she determines the qualities of the incoming and the outgoing energies, not just in relation to herself but to all selves. Contentment is constant for with the right discernment of quality comes the right use of quality and the joy of knowing the quality in all. Spiritual reading, or reading the meaning and quality in things, events, and people, is her method of discernment. And fiery aspiration impels her to be one with not only her potential dharma but with all that she may contact in fulfillment of the great law of inclusion. She is devoted to Ishvara, the soul within, the conscious quality that sparks and glows in each and every life.

This disciple knows her place in the whirling spiral. Her *asana*, or position, is that point of contact with and between other souls, spiritual compatriots in the work of evolution. Her attitude is poised in a collectivity of consciousness, aware of her brother's aspiration, dedication, strengths, weaknesses, lines of least resistance, and the upward momentum in which all find themselves.

Her *pranayama* is the breath of the spiral and of the group. Like an ashram, all share in the consciousness and vitality which is the group. The ebb and flow of the energies in her life echo the same cyclic patterns within the group and the greater group, the Hierarchy. Related to the breath of life as it is breathed by God within our planet, she increasingly becomes aware of God's solar emanations, the inhalations and exhalations of a greater level of the Lord. In sync she moves with her peers. In accommodation she moves with those she guides. With humility she moves with the Lighted Ones.

The spiral of magnetic impulse causes the disciple to withdraw from that which is extraneous or that which is not of quality and meaning. *Pratyahara* is the withdrawing of attention away from the transient and toward the real and the lasting. Now appearances fall away and characteristics of essence can be known. *Dharana* is the beginning of the process of knowing. Attentive and alert to the movement of these qualities, the disciple can learn how to use them and become an anonymous part of this concert whole. Attention is away from the not-self and fully upon the Self in all.

Then *Dhyana* - understanding, full comprehension, true meditation. No longer learning, beyond knowing, dhyana is that state of alive recognition of the facets that the whole stands revealed. In wisdom the disciple can work with the forces and energies all around him. To this goal the accepted disciple works and extends all effort. In this state of being the master works as does the soul for both are in constant meditation.

The disciple uses the heart and base chakras. The head most assuredly is engaged in those well centered. Ajna is used as a directing agent by those who know and understand . The solar plexus chakra is used by aspirants who seek to be pulled into the conscious work, and the sacral center attracts many to endeavors which are temporal but lasting in their evolutionary affect.

With the heart opening, the disciple's ears hear the pain of the world. Empathy and the acute sensing of quality and therefore of suffering are lived. Insulation is their lesson. Compassion and non attachment is their salvation.

As one increasingly walks the path of Life secondary chakras open. Hands, feet, shoulders and spine awaken to the multitude of energies and forces swirling in and through the world. Hands conduct; feet ground and elevate; shoulders that have grown stronger from the training of learning how to carry the burdens of the world, now become an arch of protection and balance. The spine is the transmittal line of powers to be used, of energies to be directed, and qualities to be given. From here the disciple bends, stands, lifts, takes, gives, kneels, conquers, and arrives.

And having arrived is initiate. In constant meditation, in ceaseless conducive tension, compassion and endless outpouring love, the initiate works in harmony with all within his radiating circumference. Though he be the center he is not. He is but another cog in the cosmic wheel.

The Second Ray of Love Wisdom and Initiates

Wisdom	Brings	Wise loving action
The wise use of slow action	Brings	Patience and rhythm
The power to save	Includes	Healing
The power of Love	Creates	Harmlessness
The power to redeem	Leads to the	Obliteration of the boundaries of ego
Radiance	Is	The revelation of Light
Love Divine	Moves through	The Savior, Bodisattva
Inclusive living and thought	Becomes	Selflessness

Figure 14

The initiates orchestrate. They play qualities like the strings of a harp. Dissonance is used to perfection; harmony results. Here is the "union of the polar opposites". Here is the wise use of all energies, all qualities, and all forces. Time is a factor to be used, but within whose hold they are held. Limitations are the boundaries constantly pushed back and expanded. We feel the pull of their purity. We are lifted by their inspiration. Drawn into the vortex of the power of their love we are transformed. All life within the three worlds is reoriented and saved. Again the words ring in our ears, "I, if I be lifted up, will draw all men unto me." How simple and profound a thought, that by the very act of one being all life can be lifted, elevated to a new spectrum of livingness. Upward, upward, round and round.

Here, the design of the seventh ray plays with the pureness of the second ray. The words of the Seventh Ray Brother as He spoke to the Second Ray Lord are most revealing. "Within the radius of the love of God, within the circle of the solar system, all forms, all souls, all lives revolve. Let each son of God enter into this wisdom. Reveal to each the oneness of the many lives."[33]

It is by interactive interplay that this oneness is revealed. It is by the momentum established as one point attracts and draws another point which draws another, which draws another, magnetically, upward, upward, round and round that life and lives are changed, reoriented, revolved, reinterpreted. Expansiveness and ultimate inclusion are the result. Nothing and no one is left out, nor do they want to be. The powerful love that emanates from the spiral of the Knowing Ones is unmistakable. Fear is completely negated. Single self is naught. What is created is Union. The poles, their opposites, and the dichotomies lived for eons can be seen as the method of madness of the not-self, the personality. Yet these same opposites and dichotomies are the tools of soul and the rites of passage on the pilgrimage to union.

The initiate is a chakra within a greater body, the body of Hierarchy and of God. Certainly various chakras are employed as the initiate works within the three worlds in the distribution, transmutation, and redirection of energies.

"Happy are the peacemakers, for they shall be called the Sons of God." Initiates at-one all that they work with and touch. Even if their task is to destroy an old form so that consciousness may indwell and use a new one, peace is brought, a "peace which passeth understanding." They are sons of God as are all illumined and enlightened people; they radiate the light of the soul which is the same as the light of God. Christ taught us to "be as is he". The Buddha assured us that he was merely "awakened" and therefore anyone else could live as such. The initiates bring together in mediation and articulation all the various qualities, be they opposites or comparatives. The peace of unified construction and whole synchronized movement is the result. They are the Sons of God.

Raja yoga and agni yoga, the yoga of fire, blend and become pure realization. They are at one with Life. They walk in meditation.

As we look to the systemic laws we fine the correspondence between the Law of Vibration and the Law of Love with this law of the soul, the

---

[33] Ibid. pg. 67.

Law of Magnetic Impulse. The Law of Vibration governs all life within the planetary system. It is the manner in which the system itself evolves. It takes account of rotary motion and the livingness of each individual spark of intelligence, recognizes the degree of conscious resolve within each appearance of quality, and empowers the beingness within all forms to express its fullest potential. Through the use of dissonance and resonance, vibration is enhanced, or keyed up, and evolution takes place, just as through dissonance and resonance vibration was encumbered, slowed, and ensheathed so that involution could occur.

One vibration plays on another; again the metaphor of the orchestra and the performance of the symphony come to mind. A violin alone cannot create the necessary tonalities and movement of sound to convey the quality that the entire orchestra can. A greater story can be told. A fuller picture is revealed.

The Law of Love is the means whereby all are lifted into this crescendo of harmony and at-one-ment. The powerful magnetism is unrelenting and all encompassing. It is a swirling embrace in which individual identity is lost and whole identification is entered. Love pulses, beats, and causes the momentum of the spiral. Impulse beats within us, causing movement and eventual momentum. Until we move at the speed of light - the light of soul.

Chapter Four
The Third Law of the Soul
The Law of Service
"The Law of the Water and Fishes"

What is service? Helping a child learn to read or write; assisting an elderly person with their housework or errands; giving money to a charity; working for something that is politically or philosophically important to one? All these might be examples that people would give of how they serve. What about being clergy, a volunteer at a hospital, or doing a stint with Habitat for Humanity or Peace Corps? Is service separate from the rest of one's life? And is service understood by the soul the same as that which the personality calls service?

The Law of Service is a window into the reality of soul's instinct to assist, empower, and release. Through it we peer seeing how the soul choices of work and the revelation of its desires. Listening to stories of service rendered we hear these demonstrated. The Law of Service is a law that speaks of the fundamental standing of the soul in matter, the ways in which soul temporarily lives within that confine, and of the ways of its self-achieved release. All this soul does simultaneously illumining to others the path of their release.

Service is an outward movement from soul to the soul in another body or form. This simple gesture reaches out to the light of consciousness enveloped in sheaths of matter. There soul meets its counterpart on the field of experience and on the shared plane of activity. Soul bends or stretches to accommodate and adapt to the need of the moment. Both souls are touched by the genuine-ness of the giving and by the experience lived. The origin of this motion is inclusion, an automatic desire of the soul. With this we recognize that inclusion will work both ways requiring attentiveness to what is being given as well as to what is being asked.

Service is an energy exchange, compatible, and engendering. It is about need and fulfillment, asana and tension. Service is not about abundance or sentimentality, or about good intentions. It is work done and done to the best of one's abilities in the moment and in life.

Service acknowledges that one has something to give and that one knows what that something is. This she gives in fullness, openness, and willfulness. Service is knowing one's niche and filling it, while being content to do so.

Service is ongoing, unending once consciously begun. One act creates or leads to the next act of service. All these begin to fill the awakening mind with complexity; yet soul sees the activity as one simple wide movement, like a sweeping embrace. But to what purpose?

Service is the means by which soul is put in contact with all forms of life. Through service and the learning experiences of serving, soul is put in touch with quality in forms and all levels of matter. Thus it observes how that particular quality moves in that matter. Through experience soul has learned how to liberate aspects of itself and now through cooperative experience can attempt to teach this liberating process to other souls in form. Minimally, light is seen and nurtured through the fostering of service. Maximally, a degree of conscious liberation takes place and that awakened one will go out and serve.

Service attunes the personality to the desires and needs of the soul. Soul desires its tools (the vehicles of the personality) to work well in the worlds of form. Personality seeks its own expression. The two are blended through service as the personality, with its strengths, abilities, and personal (and often correct) motivations are coordinated with the soul's wise understanding of need. Through the experience of service, the personality learns to see itself as part of an outreaching whole. Personality feels included and empowered, and opens up to self-examination and personal growth processes. Thus are each of the vehicles brought into a higher state of refinement and into a more resonant relation with each other. This becomes another act of service - a service of the self to its wholeness.

Service is also a point where space and time meet. The wise use of time is a necessity in service. There is much that needs to be done from the observant eye of soul. One incarnation is not a lot of time. Soul does have the advantage of understanding continuity, but the time is ever at hand for action and right effort. Space is the area of its dynamic work. Space is the medium through which magnetic cooperation occurs. And space is the end result of service. In other words, as a result of service the soul radiates more and therefore fills more space with its being; and the one served also shines to a greater degree, hence the same result.

True service is delicate and often goes unnoticed, for that's how subtle the need can be. Also some of the service ongoing in the world today is subjective, in realms unseen, and therefore barely perceived. Yet, service is vivifying, alert, and commanding. It breaks down walls, calls like a trumpet to the sleeping consciousness, and grasps the outstretched hand. True service is no mistake. It is willful, direct, and on target. It is masterful, artistic, and uplifting. Service is inspirational and calls us to aspire together, a league of hearts and hands, mindful of one another.

The Sixth Ray of Idealism and Devotion moves through the Law of Service. This ray distributes the energy of the Ideal, the Possible and the Perfect Model, State, or Vision of anything. It is the energy that moves us towards that goal and objective. The Ideal is always outside of us, just beyond our reach or state of achievement. It is to be sought, reached for, striven after. All of these qualities are sixth ray qualities in humanity. The understanding of the reach leads to encouragement, inspiration, and aspiration. To cheer someone on, to support with the words, "you can do it," is the sixth ray in action whether said to a baby learning to walk or an adult with depression.

This ray provides upward movement. It aspires toward the sun, the light, and the lighter side of life. In the plant kingdom it gives the ability to grow upward and outward; to, as a seed, push dirt and small stones out of the way and emerge into the light of day. In a human being it gives us the ability to take things lightly, not stay angry, depressed, or hurt for long, but instead to bounce back.

The Rays are archetypal. They are energy streams, breaths of the Divine. As such, each ray provides much to all life. Often, as people learn of the rays they think mostly in terms of how the ray affects, conditions, and moves within an individual and the human family. This is similar to limiting consideration of the animal kingdom to domesticated animals and forgetting about insects, fish, birds, and everything else that comprise the animal kingdom. So, in contemplating a Ray, we do so first as an energy, then consider examples of its expression.

The Sixth Ray is also the ray of devotion, understood as a divine energy stream, therefore is different from devotion lived by most people. Devotion is the act of giving, to the point of losing self in the wholeness of a larger or more transcendent self. Devotion is the supreme desire. The world scriptures give many examples of the devotion of Deity to create, support, and give totally to that which It created. Krishna says in the Bhagavad Gita, "I am the father of this universe, the mother, the sustainer, and the grandsire… I am the same toward all beings."[34] The Book of Wisdom states, "The spirit of the Lord, indeed fills the whole world."[35]

Devotion is the other side of the coin of Transcendence, therefore the sixth ray is the ray of transcendence. The Second ray of Love Wisdom is the ray of Immanence. Transcendence, on the other hand, is an ideal. It is the perfected Deity, the Most High, the Absolute. Transcendence is outside of a person, like the sun is outside the growing plant. The plant is fed by sunlight. But not all people are fed by this relationship with the Divine. Some are left quite alone, with the feeling of abandon and lack of self-worth. These too are sixth ray qualities.

Devotion as it moves into the human kingdom takes on the accoutrements we are familiar with: self-negation, dependency, jealousy, specialness, loyalty, to name a few. Devotees of all religions and sects share the sixth ray. Devotion means that what is important or meaningful to one person should be meaningful to everyone else, so truth becomes "my truth". Consider all the extreme or heinous things done in the name of truth, belief, or conviction. The sixth ray is all of these working with and through humanity.

Devotion is parenthood, the presidency, or being the UN Secretary General. Devotion to a cause, an ideal, political bent, religion or atheism,

---

[34] *Bhagavad Gita*, 9: 17, 29.
[35] Book of Wisdom, 1:7

to a person or alma mater are all forms of devotion. The mystical experience of relation to and with the Divine is as ancient as people's prayer life. People around the world know that this is possible and that it has been experienced by many. The losing of oneself in ecstasy or bliss in the embrace of Sophia (Solomon), Krishna (Hari Krishna), Ahura Mazda (Zoroaster), Christ (the Christian mystics), Buddha nature (Nirvana), in the embrace of the Sun (Sun dance), or the Mother Earth (Sweat Lodge or Kiva) these are part of the human existence, of being "in this world and not of it."

Extremism is often a part of the demonstration of the Sixth Ray. To be for or against, impassioned or disdainful, to love or hate a person or thing, to put someone or something on a pedestal and then to be crushed when the pedestal falls down and the person turns out to be just like anyone else with strengths and weaknesses are all tendencies of the sixth ray in humanity.

Figure 15
The Sixth Ray of Idealism and Devotion

Idealism	is born of	The Pure, the lofty, the most sublime
Transcendence	embraces	The Seeker and the Sought
Upliftment	is	The power to salvage
Faith	brings	Fearlessness born of Trust
Vision, visionary	results in	Ideals revealed
Devotion	relates	Each to each other, the many to the One
Imperishable	becomes	Undeterred
Innocence	is	Upholder of Truth

The workings of any law of the soul must be seen in the context of the group. So although we can readily pick out people who are serving and giving what might be called true service we must look to the greater groups of the masses, the disciples, and the initiates to see this law in its own light and not in the light of the individual. Also we can look at the mineral and vegetable kingdoms because there we easily see this law at work. Through these two kingdoms we additionally see how closely linked the Law of Service is to the Law of Sacrifice.

The sacrifice of the mineral kingdom is to confine itself in the most rigid of forms, to evolve in a way almost imperceptible to the human eye, and yet it is in this way and as a service that it becomes the very fiber of our exoteric being. We are built out of the mineral kingdom. It is our substance and our foundation. We can materialize because the Entity Whose body of expression is the mineral kingdom chose to sacrifice Himself upon the cross of matter. His sacrifice becomes His service. All life can evolve through form because the mineral kingdom serves as the medium. So subtle, so unobtrusive is this reality that humanity has taken this fact for granted. Were it not for the mineral kingdom souls could not incarnate into physical forms and gain and learn from the experiences of those incarnations. Were it not for the service of the mineral kingdom soul would not be able to touch and taste the delicacies of the material world. The solid shake of a hand, the colors at sunset, the majesty and power of a volcano, all are because of the mineral kingdom and its service to the Planetary Lord. Our bones are made of it, our food is salted by it, our roads, buildings, cars, boats, planes, and space shuttles are made of the stuff of the mineral kingdom.

The sacrifice of the vegetable kingdom is to be the sustenance of the world. In so sacrificing Itself, the vegetable kingdom began its eons of service. The food chain begins with the plant eaters and from there all other animals, including humans, gain their nourishment. The earth's atmospheric system is dependent upon this kingdom. And the human sense of aesthetics has much to do with the vegetable kingdom. Beauty is a great service and gift that the plant kingdom gives. The palette of God is fresh with the colors that will become flowers, fruits, and a canopy of leaves. Our eyes can feast. Our nostrils can breathe both fresh and perfumed air as the plants and flowers work and serve. We are nourished and fed. We are cleansed and healed by the service of the vegetable kingdom.

The plant kingdom also teaches us the wise use of time as its lives are lived out in cycles of seasons, cold and hot, dry and wet, dormant and vitally alive. Plants of the daylight, plants of the night, all teach us to make the most of each moment, ray of light, and drop of rain. "Maximize and aspire" could be the motto of the plant world, for it does both exceedingly well; and teaches both quietly, earnestly, unmistakably.

One piece of humanity's act of service upon this planet is to grow the light of mind from instinct into awareness; by doing this mind will become consciousness. As the midway point in the kingdoms upon this earth[36], humanity is the bridge between the lower realms of instinctual intelligence and the higher planes of universal mind-consciousness. A service of the masses is to be the petrie dish of that great scientist, God. The masses are the medium into which the germ of intelligence was placed. Given reasonable conditions, through education, governance, societal norms, and religions that intelligence grows. Growing in the individual, all of the masses grow and change. The change is usually slow, even cumbersome. Occasionally, however, it is dramatic. An example of this would be the invention of the printing press in the Western hemisphere[37] and therefore the introduction of printed matter into the hands of the masses as well as the elite. No doubt, progress was slow before average people were included in the privilege of learning how to read and write, but once that was established as a societal practice there was no turning back. The spark of intelligence was being fanned. Its glow is now unmistakable.

Another example of dramatic change came with the evidence that the sun is the center of our solar system. In establishing this, the thinkers of the race created a space in which a person could question authority, his religion and its dogmas, his relation to his god, his fellow human being, and even his relation to the earth. Science decreed that the church, and therefore much of the prevalent culture, was not in line with the real or with the irrefutable facts. In questioning authority the masses began independent thought, thought apart from the dictates of the elite. In questioning the absoluteness of the religious doctrines, mankind was left to wonder

---

[36] There are seven kingdoms upon this planet from the esoteric perspective. Three below – mineral, plant, and animal, the human, and three above the human – Hierarchy/the kingdom of souls, angelic or devic kingdom, and planetary beings.

[37] The Chinese had been printing texts since the 2nd century AD.

as much as to think. Wondering employs the creative imagination, and that eventually stretches to reach the plane of higher mind; thus a link was forged between the three aspects of Mind (concrete mind, soul, abstract mind). A light began to shine forth in humanity. It does so steadily still.

Service is also rendered daily by the masses in the work done with the three worlds of form. Though we so often see the ways of humanity to be contrary to the ways of God, that perspective stems from a view of the part and not of the whole. Via humanity's work the mineral kingdom has experienced a release or liberation on a scale unseen in millions of years. The use of fire, water, and air, as well as the use of the power of impact has forced the mineral kingdom to respond. Up until the very recent decades the only external influences exerted upon the mineral kingdom have been from the earth herself, the sun, and occasional meteorites. Now a radiation, a throwing off of that which enshrines the life essence of this kingdom, is taking place at a rate that is fantastic.

With the vegetable kingdom mankind feels very at home. The masses revel in the seeming abundance offered by and procured from this kingdom. Through hybridization and farming, and the cultivation of herbs and plants for homeopathic, naturapathic and wholistic medicines, the evolution of the vegetable kingdom has also been stepped up. This kingdom, like the mineral, has been forced to live in accordance with a will other than its own and the earth's.[38] Mankind uses plant life to decorate his surroundings with gardens, personal greenhouses, and indoor plants. Man has become an artist, the vegetable kingdom his paint. And through the use of the vegetable kingdom for food and health (inner and outer), individual species have flowered into a fuller expression and use of their divine intention. The essence of the vegetable kingdom shines forth as humanity comes to appreciate it in multiple ways. Granted all has not been perfectly executed, and both the mineral and vegetable kingdoms have seen setbacks but these are temporary and not at all on a scale similar to the expansion and release of the consciousness of these kingdoms.

---

[38] There is much apparent negative interaction with the plant kingdom as well, such as deforestation and the loss of uncataloged plant life.

The Sixth Ray of Idealism and Devotion and the Masses

Naiveté	becomes	Innocence
Gullibility	Leads to	A believer, a follower, often without thought
Spontaneous	Leads to	Impulsive
Self-sacrificing	Leads to	Needing to be acknowledged or recognized
Buoyancy	Brings	Positive attitude
Reactive, quick to emote	Leads to	Personalizing
Hope	Leads to	Trust
Easily disappointed	Leads to	Anger

Figure 16

    The solar plexus is the chakra of personal interaction, and of how we feel about things, people, and ourselves to a large extent. It is our primary seat of psychic awareness, that is to say, the feeling of shared existence. Service is so much about our feeling nature until the soul is the primary mover in the worlds. We serve because we feel it will make things better. We serve to give ourselves something to do that is wholesome and right. We serve because we feel guilty. The solar plexus is related to all of these.

    Solar plexus is the chakra where the most connection and interaction of feeling and mind takes place. Therefore, as an individual learns to think more clearly, one is freer from the pulls of the emotions and how they affect thought. Thus, the individual can serve more effectively. Also, since the Law of Service is actually a law of the soul, it will be only as the clarified mind is the primary instrument of the person, and not the tides of the emotional nature, that the soul's service can begin in the world. For example, a woman might be a Girl Scout leader for years, teaching young girls to feel good about themselves and to help in their community. For that person, this might be soul service. It could be, though, that those years with the Girls Scouts were training for a wider service in a larger community that would span many cities and across national borders. The first might have been service that trained the personality to be aligned with the patience and light of the soul and so give that freely to the children. The second will require the established posture (asana) of alignment so that the light and wisdom of the soul will pour through in words, teaching, and deeds.

Service also employs the heart and throat chakras. Heart provides the sense of inclusion, and wanting to participate in something because one knows it is the right thing to do, regardless of hardship, whether other people agree or not, or the constraints of time. But make no mistake, where there is heart there is clear mind. The heart is not gushy or sentimental, nor is it pulled into things that are un-soul oriented. The heart is heart-mind. It includes wisdom and a knowing that is not based on psychic feelings about this or that, but instead on a deep understanding. The heart is not impulsive, but is decisive. The heart is intent and seeks to unmask divine intention through avenues of service.

Throat chakra relates to intelligence, creativity, and expression in the worlds. Service is a combination of all of these. Service requires different things at different times from everyone. The throat chakra, being primarily associated with the mind , thought processes, time and its cycles, helps us move intelligently, resourcefully, and pre-meditatively.

The combination of throat, heart, and solar plexus opens realms of possibilities contained within our self that are as yet un, or not fully expressed. These three chakras align the individual with the Abstract Mind and the Mind of God. We are struck by an idea that would better, that would empower or release some one or some thing. Maybe it is an idea that would just make things simpler. This is service. And how it works out in the world (our families, workplaces, and global community) will be determined by which of the three chakras is most highly functioning or the even-ness shared between all three. If solar plexus is the main focal point, the service will be more self-serving; with throat in the forefront, the service will tend towards idea implementation and at first a scatteredness that might derail the person or the project; with heart in the lead the person could step into an act of service that is too big or overwhelming for what the person actually can offer and sustain. With all three in equal measure and full operation any project will go forward efficiently, rhythmically, being inspired from the solar plexus, thought through with clarity from the throat, and empowered by the magnetism, courage, and independence of the all inclusive heart.

The gregariousness of the sixth ray is at work within the masses. People want to belong or be lead along. There is also appreciation and incremental refinement due to this ray's relation to purity. The need to give and to be given to are hallmarks of the even numbered rays (2, 4, 6), especially the sixth and second. Both are at work and move the masses toward the common goal of betterment and right relations.

We can see humanity using some of the Buddha's Eightfold Path. Right effort, right livelihood, and right action seem to be at work. Streaming out of the idealism of this ray there is the desire to do better and to create better for the children of the world. The motive is pure enough; the effort substantial.

Livelihoods are being chosen with some forethought in the more affluent and educated countries (vision, a quality of the sixth ray). Careers are embarked upon which hold not only advancement but often enjoyment and prosperity for the individual.

Right action is constantly being tested, revised, and tested again. In this fast changing world of mixing cultures and ideas the context of right action is ever changing. It requires flexibility and an openness to all that experience has to offer. Children are being raised differently than they were thirty years ago. Many are being taught the concept of right action by their parents and their schools.

The disciple, by definition, has a greater degree of Self-consciousness. As such he sees his abilities and his contribution with relative clarity. He can now give and in giving serve. In giving his time he serves the moment. In giving his mind he serves the quest for greater understanding. In giving his thoughts he serves the growing mind of humanity. In giving his strengths and his weaknesses he serves the power of humility and the fragility of the human psyche. In giving his spirit he serves Spirit. In giving his heart he serves the common good.

Humility is an interesting quality: a combination of soft confidence and surety born of simply being. Humility is gentle because the harshness of ego is gone; self-referencing and self-importance is replaced with wise presence. The humble person can get much done because people want to work with this co-worker. There is respect for her or him.

The Sixth Ray of Idealism and Devotion and Disciples

Self-referencing	Creates its opposite	Humility
Self-negation	Leads to	Consecration
Seeking	Becomes	Gratitude
Listening	Opens to	Guidance
Undeterred	Develops into	Persistence
Doubt	Is turned around	Conviction
Aspiration	Becomes	Ardor
Fiery Will	Ensures	Goals Achieved
Loyalty	Develops into	Co-worker

Figure 17

Little by little the disciple gives more and more until all is consecrated in the simple gesture of service. Self-negation is a quality of the sixth ray, and often one that is not empowering to the average person. It easily becomes the source of self-worth issues, self-criticism, and self-judgment. Self-negation is born, however, from a divine tendency: to put others first. It also streams from the sixth ray quality of abstraction, the ability to move up and out of self. That vantage point is faulty until the soul has permeated the separating mind. The extremism of the sixth ray turns habits and qualities into black and white statements of good and bad. When the soul is the observer, all is seen as the progressive state of purification and betterment that it is, and not freeze-framed as a forever state of lack.

The quality of consecration unveils how the Law of Sacrifice and the Law of Service are inextricably linked. In time the personality gives to the soul and becomes its servant. In so doing it becomes a master over itself. The personality stands redeemed, a master of the three worlds which for uncounted lives held him in bondage. As servant of the soul he becomes servant of the soul in all.

Service is the seeker and the sought finding each other, not by serendipity or chance, but by synchronicity and magnetic need. The disciple is learning, often through trial and error, the right distribution of energies and the right use of force. Listening to the voice of the silence within his heart, he becomes aware of the need at hand. If his duty lies there it pulls like a magnet. The moment is alive with the electricity of soul, of will needing to manifest. In this instance how can there be doubt as to the right course of action.

The reality is that often there is doubt for the disciple. Questioning the need, the resources, the law of the greater good, he stands motionless. Quandaries about harmlessness, right speech, and right action crowd the mind. Fear of failure, the opinion of others, and even fear of success holds the disciple inactive. This position of apparent inertia is so important. Soul understands that not all situations are to be corrected by one earnest disciple. There are avenues for dharma, and avenues for karma. There are also times when the need of the brother or sister is to work things out on their own. Here we touch on the crux of service for the disciple: responsibility.

It has been said that with increased awareness comes increased responsibility. It is also safe to say that with increased awareness comes the necessity to serve. As awareness increases the disciple cannot dismiss the very real weight and feeling of responsibility. Frequently this is a test and the disciple must see clearly through it so that his real responsibility can take precedence over his perceived burden. The perceived burden is well pictured in the symbol for Aquarius, The World Server. Upon his shoulder he holds a pitcher pouring out the waters of Life. His back is slightly bent supporting the weight of the ever-flowing vessel. While his hands hold the vessel he can do little else with them. His hands are not free to help or to serve. But when the burden of responsibility, like the vessel of water, is lifted up to his head and set to rest upon the crown chakra, it is a burden no more. The sense of responsibility becomes accepted will. There is no longer fear of failure or success; no longer a feeling of weight. The personal self, the vessel of the soul, has been levitated to its rightful positions.

The hands now free can work the magic of service. Recognizing a need, and that it is his to fill, the disciple employs discrimination, so that only that which is required is done; no more, no less. The conscious disciple will not take upon himself that which is others to do, that which is their opportunity for learning, growth and experience. The knowing worker will, with skillful artistry, use all at his command to fulfill soul's desire to serve.

Symbols again reveal much. This time we look at the symbol for the Law of Service. It is the vessel of water set upon the head, not held in the hands. From there it can be measured out according to need. While on the shoulder, the waters poured forth indiscriminately, some receiving according to their need, some were flooded, and others received not nearly enough. Trying to serve all, the would-be server did almost as much damage as good. Yet from atop the head the soul, knowing the soul in all, gives only that which fosters the many.

Asana marks the attitude and the posture of the disciple. Totally present and attentive to the needs of the moment the disciple stands ready. His attitude is one of dynamic flow. The soul controls; the personality whole-heartedly responds. His stance changes with the demands on his time, heart, mind, and psyche. Malleable and adaptive, yet completely resolute, the disciple is poised and balanced.

The entire Eightfold Path is employed in the various means of service offered by the disciple. Certainly the servers are the "humble" of the Beatitudes and the "treasures" which they will inherit are the seeds of goodness and light set, grown, and harvested by the laws of karma. Humbly they will witness the changes in the world that they helped to create through service.

Disciples employ the heart, throat, ajna, and head chakras primarily. The heart is in touch with the pulse of life in form. The throat moves the disciple through a wide variety of creative experiences and helps him maintain rhythm between that which seeks expression and the completeness of the expression. Ajna sees the need, as does the heart, in the context of the real and in the vision of the whole. The head (crown) chakra ensures that the awakened disciple serves the essence of soul and of the Plan, and does so in forethought and conscious knowing.

The third ray of Active Intelligence and Adaptability is at work as well as the sixth ray within the ranks of the disciples. Adapting to the needs of the times, pliable to the changing energies of her co-workers, yet firmly rooted in the basic instinct to serve and touch the worlds, the disciple moves in many circles finding her niche in each. Service is like a three-dimensional mobile hanging from a string. Each part balances the other parts. As each level or layer moves the other levels are moved. Through the inter-related achievement of balance and motion the mobile is a piece of physical beauty. So is service. Service works with the inner beauty, the inner divinity, as well as with the outer pronunciations of that beauty.

Understanding the undulations of time, initiates work with the potential of beauty and the potency of hidden qualities, thus touching the essences held within matter. With ultimate simplicity they work. Desiring the most whole result, they see the direct route their energies should take as well as the most profitable investment of time. This law is basically about "give and take" and the initiates know exactly what they give, to what degree it should be given, and what the take or result will be. They, as soul itself, are never drained dry of life-giving waters, but certain of their energies can be temporarily tapped as they work within the three-worlds. As part of give and take, they also know how to take or rather invoke that which is needed to ensure adequate supply of quality, energy, and dynamic interplay so that service and its end result are accomplished.

The Sixth Ray of Idealism and Devotion and Initiates

Vision of Reality	Leads to	Conscious interaction of the higher and lower realms of consciousness
To Uphold Truth	Leads to	Reverence
Fearless	Leads to	Ceaseless
Power to Detach Oneself	Leads to	Freedom from personalization
Power to Overcome the Hold and Pulls of the emotional nature	Leads to	Freedom to use the Waters of Life

Figure 18

As initiates stand free of the bonds of matter, they are likewise free to stand in matter. In doing so they touch, uplift, redeem, transform, and spiritualize matter. During that process they continue to gain the subtle experiences that only matter can give. Touched they learn more of the pull into it; and touching they realize release. Then as magicians they serve through wielding energies and reaching out to consciousness incarnate.

At this point of evolution master and servant become equal terms. The master knows and so He serves. The servant has learned and so has become wise and harmless in all exchanges of energy. Following the radiant aura and the wise teachings of a master, many would serve Him or Her. In the end, however, they serve something greater. Following, humanity down the ages has been brought to new levels of awareness thus creating new areas of service that in turn uplift the state of existence of life on this planet. Service leads to redemption and is the work of salvation.

Here again we call the initiates "the pure of heart, the peacemakers, and the merciful." They are the knowing Sons and Daughters of God who work to bring light into clearer view for all to see. All means of Raja Yoga are used in their work. They are harmless and so can serve in every capacity. They are purified and so can work at purifying matter. They are in rhythm with the breaths of God and so can flow with the tides of involution and evolution, embodiment and dissolution. Their stance is one of power and being, love and dedication, in common, in unanimity, in harmony with the Plan of God. Attentive and withdrawn, they use the three worlds unhampered and unattached. And resonating with the word incarnate, the soul in form, they utter words divine calling out to the light ensheathed and cause it to stir.

The sixth ray of renewal, rebirth, desire, qualified love, devotion, and the recognition of the ideal is at work at this level of understanding. On the highest turn of the spiral the sixth ray employs the act of refinement and assessment of the most subtle and pure. In this way all nuances can be used and not wasted. All qualities can be expressed with the betterment of the whole its result. But this is done through the delicate art of sensitive direction. Fullness is the end result.

There is a story of the Buddha who, after a few days of not seeing one of his students and noticing as well that the student's chores were not being done, inquired about this. A teaching disciple replied that the student was sick and had been for the last few days. The Buddha then asked who was attending him and was answered that no one was since it was obvious that this student had taken ill as a result of karma. The Buddha in silence left and found the ill student lying in his own vomit and excrement, weak from fever and lack of food and water.

Buddha lovingly bathed and fed the chela and then proceeded to wash down the room, the bed and the student's clothes. He tended him day and night.

After a couple of days the disciple went looking for his Master and found Him in the room of the chela, nursing the now rallying student. The disciple was astonished and ashamed and asked the Lord Buddha if he could help so that the Lord would not be subjected to such lowly tasks. The Buddha bade him go and meditate on who the disciple seeks to serve and why, and then meditate on who he chose not to.

Service runs the gamut from the most menial of tasks to the most subjective. All are equally important. All must be done.

The Law of Service emanates out of the cosmic Law of Economy which governs all instinctual natures. It is the instinct of the soul to serve, help, and better the forms that express quality and consciousness. As has been said, true service is done with exactitude, knowing the needs of the moment and accomplishing just that. Economy of time, motion, words and energy are pre-requisites to service.

The systemic of Magnetic Control stands out as a correspondent of the Law of Service. Magnetic Control slowly brings the personality into resonance with the soul. Rhythmically and through the powerful energies of attraction and wisdom, the soul impresses the vehicles of the personality, thus anchoring itself in form, and then coordinates them into a workable whole. Over time the personality feels itself as hollow and lacking. Then the soul seizes the opportunity to impress the personality with its presence, harmony, and loving powerful design. Little by little the personality feels that these two aspects of the self, the seen and the unseen, are created to be as one. At that point the personality invites the ways of the soul and the two work toward union.

Service, like the Law of Magnetic Control, is about resonance. Magnetically and electrically people, groups, nations, and kingdoms are brought together to help one another and further the Plan held in the mind of God. The Law of Magnetic Control acknowledges all aspects of the personality nature - its instincts, tendencies, aspirations, fears, and joys - and utilizes them bringing the personality into a new and refined state of being. Service ever brings us to the next step simultaneously readying us to take it. Service is the training ground and is the next responsibility where our training will be tested. We are stretched by service, as we enter into new expressions of the soul seeking to touch the world in more expansive ways. Thus are we expanded. Life is expressed. Matter is served and its essential divine nature revealed.

Faith and trust develop into conviction and a powerful presence as servers, challenged by new spheres of responsibility, discipline themselves and work for the greater good. Hearts, minds, and hands move in unison as service is rendered. Stories are told of hands that helped so many, hearts full and giving, and of minds alive with teachings simple enough for a child to understand. Service brings us together, just as it first brought the vehicles of the personality together and then brought together the personality and soul. With each touch lives are altered and seen anew. With each insight the urge to serve grows stronger. With each attempt at service we understand more how truly to serve.

Service destroys illusions, often attracts attention, employs all our knowledge and requires heart. Service is analytical and always critical to the moment, as we assess if it is our moment and our service. Service is the stance of the warrior of light, the worker in the three worlds of form. Service is redeeming, purifying, dedicated, unswerving, and resolute. Service is magic and the server a magician who can re-route rivers, grow lotuses in the most arid of existences, tame the wild and give strength to the down-trodden. Service empowers, acknowledges, and enlightens. Service changes everything it touches. It is the touch of soul.

Chapter Five
The Fourth Law of the Soul
The Law of Repulse
"The Law of All Destroying Angels"

When the essence of someone or something is pure and vibrant the Law of Repulse has been at work. When a being's presence is vital and lends to the coherence of the whole the Law of Repulse has been the integrating factor. When resonance rings through a form, resounding the signature intonation that is the form, as well as the consciousness that indwells it and the spirit symbolized by that signature, the Law of Repulse has been engaged. When definition, design, detail, and identity stand revealed, Repulse, most sacred Repulse, has been the tool.

Our understanding of this word is so limited. When we first look at the word repulse we are ourselves repulsed, afraid of what it might draw to our attention. We see repulse in one context, that which is lesser, unredeemed, unworthy, and unattractive. Yet at the core of the Law of Repulse is wisdom and compassion. This law will bring every conscious life to a door of recognition and therefore to a door of passage. Repulse is the ritual and the rite of that passage. Atom to man, snowflake to ocean, each vehicle to each plane of being, each must use the Law of Repulse or else stagnation will be their destiny. Lack of clarity and the resultant lack of coherence will be their demise. How loving is repulse; how vital and evolutionary this law.

The Law of Repulse states that that which is not one's own shall be rejected, that which is not in line with the decree of the soul shall be negated. Individuality and individualism are born as the recognition of that which is "me" and that which is not takes root. Individuality is sensing the lines demarking self and other. It is knowing that there are others and that they are not "me." Individuality bears the fruit of definition and uniqueness as the person learns more and more what is him and his and what is the other and theirs.

The Law of Repulse is the great separator. Because of repulse lines are drawn around, between, and even through. In this way all forms, including the so-called formless, have a definite place in space in which they hold their presence. All vehicles, planes of being, and all kingdoms have definition and a ring-pass-not because repulse ensures the separation of each from another. Repulse requires that each vehicle vibrate to a particular rate that can be enhanced and heightened but may not exceed a particular threshold. It would then become something else, vibrating to a different rate, something that has a different place in space and reason for being.

A better understanding might be gained through a look at the human vehicles (mental, emotional, etheric/physical) and their corresponding planes of existence. Each vehicle vibrates to and at a particular frequency. Each vehicle has its particular resonance or sound wave. That wave is distinct, finite and self-contained. Each vehicle has overriding hues peculiar only to that vehicle. These are not the rays of a person's *constitution*[39] but the coloration of the vehicle itself. All humans would have these colorations, as they are a determinant of the vehicle in question. The vibration, sound, and coloration of a vehicle correspond to the energy pulsating through the affiliated plane of existence. For instance, an etheric sheath would have the overriding quality of the seventh ray, the ray of etheric substance, even though the ray being used by the incarnated soul personalizing that vehicle could well be different. An astral (emotional) vehicle will have the overriding vibration of the sixth ray, designating it as the astral vehicle, and separating it from any and all other vehicles because the astral plane vibrates to or is an expression of the sixth ray. The ray coloration being used during incarnation by soul will likewise stand revealed as the vehicle itself maintains its integrity and definition and the ray currently in use retains its specific vibration and coloration.

---

[39] Constitution – our three bodies plus the personality coordinating them, understood as a whole.

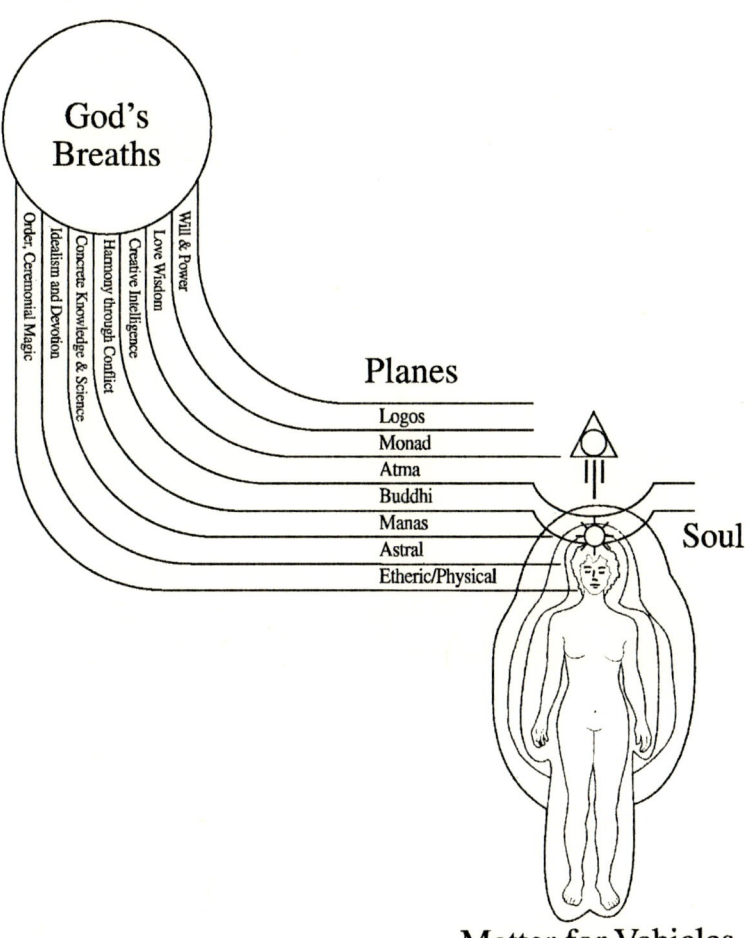

Figure 19

There are options of ray upon a vehicle from which the incarnating soul can chose. This is largely determined by one's point on the Path of Evolution.

Soul - any ray
Personality - any ray
Mental - 5, 4, 1, 3, 7, 2 in order of percentages[40]
Astral - 6, 2, 1, 4
Physical - 3, 7, 1, 6

---

[40] Certain rays are rare upon particular vehicles, such as ray 2 on the mind. They are listed in order of their frequency of choice by souls as they incarnate.

So although the ray conditioning a plane of matter was established by Deity's outbreath long ago, human souls can further condition the particular matter in question (an astral or mental vehicle, for example) with more specificity.[41]

The vibration or pulse of one vehicle, or one plane, creates a boundary or ring-pass-not. Because of this, as an example, the astral plane cannot slip into the mental plane. The ring-pass-not is the affect of the on-going repulse of one designed integrity from another. Therefore, planes are integrity at work. Their wholeness and individuality along with their separate functioning is the fulcrum on which all existence stands. All forms of life are destined to move through each plane of being and know each vehicle of expression. This is the Grand Design. And it is through the cyclic pattern of attraction and repulse that this takes place.

The planes function according to the first four means to yoga. Through yama they take nothing that is not their own. In so doing each plane is harmless to all other planes and thereby to itself. Through nijama it purifies and resents anything that is not part of its design. Resent is the term to use, considering it as two words, re-sent. Anything that is not related to the definition of that plane is sent back to its origin. Each plane is in constant tension re-informing all aspects of itself to the point of eventual sublime purification.

The pranayama of a plane of being is its pulsation and the ceaseless intonation of its word of existence. This breath is the source of, and at the same time, the vibratory rate, coloration, and the word incarnate of the plane. This breath is specific and unique. It is intrinsic to only that one plane, like the scent of a person is intrinsic to only that person. And like the breath, it is whole within itself, self mobilized and self-actuated.

This self-mobilization is the asana taken by the plane within its ring-pass-not. It stands in space, formed to a particular design, destined to hold that stance for the duration of its purposeful breathing; all this because it repulses any and all that is not conforming to its design.

---

[41] For example, I am a Second ray soul, with a 6th ray personality, 1st ray mental body, 2nd ray astral body, and 3rd ray physical body.

Consider the word design. It speaks of a definite plan, an articulated desire, and a conscious undertaking. Design is very selective, with nothing done arbitrarily or by accident. Design considers method, material, time, and space. It considers dimension and longevity. Design chooses, but chooses as much by that which is not needed, required, or wanted, as by what is; for example, the process of a snowflake taking on shape. Five snowflakes will have very distinct shapes and contours. Each design is exquisitely unique. The awareness of the snowflake actively repulses the water molecules in a way to create a line here, cavity there, an arch here, triangle there. Attraction has already pulled together the matter from which the snowflake would create its desired form. Now, in order to create that which is its own form, it repels any matter, or in this case water, that will not fit into its preordained design. Intentionally, artistically, and perfectly, knowing that it has only one chance during this incarnation of a snowstorm, the snowflake repulses, creates, and gives glory to the One.

Design and definition are the hallmarks of all forms. Both are possible only because of repulse. Design is fitting matter into the appropriate place. Design is staying true to the original intention. Design is dimensional purpose.

Definition goes hand-in-hand with design. Definition is knowing what something is and what it is not, what it is designed for and what not, what its duration is, and its resolve. To define something is to know all these. Criteria must be satisfied and that which is not necessary be negated. By definition we know something. Definitions conjure images; definitions are very tidy rings-pass-not. Definition also *becomes* the ring-pass-not of something's verity and existence because anything not pertaining to the intended sojourn in space-time is repulsed, not included. This brings clarity and integrity to the design. In the end, that which separated and repulsed has been the avenue of cohesion.

Species have definition. Kingdoms have definition. Vehicles, planes of realization, and people, all have definition. There is a definite step out of one kingdom into another. A chrysanthemum is not a bird. There is no gray area. Likewise within a kingdom there is clear distinction. An indigo beetle is not a house cat. For people there is definite demarcation between the physical body and the mental body (incorrectly called the mind by many). Saturn's planetary design and intention is very different from Mercury's or Jupiter's. There is no doubt and no overlap. This is repulse in action. Demarcation, definition, species identification, and orbital progressions are all a result of repulse. A drop of rain as it falls through the atmosphere retains its shape and molecular structure because of repulse. It might absorb additional ingredients on its way down through attraction but it does not diffuse into something else. It remains a raindrop. Repulse.

Repulse is concerned with the refinement of vibration, which in turn is the refinement of quality. Pulse is vibration. Pulse is the *Word* reverberating in space. Pulse is rhythmic in time and is constant. Re-pulse is to beat to the conscious desire of deity, clearer, truer. As the intention of soul repeats, as the word incarnate resounds (re-sounds), that which is not in alignment or enhancing the process of the spiritualization of matter is sent forth to be picked up and used by another whose purpose this material will enhance. Through repetition comes perfection. Through the repetition of the word, or pulse, the various aspects of the self see clearly their place and part in the grand design of soul. In the same manner soul sees its place and part in the Grand Design of monad and God. Planetary purposes unfold, intentions of Kingdoms are defined, done largely by seeing what they are not.

Repulse has for eons kept various aspects of the human kingdom separate. Coming out of the animal kingdom we kept the sense of species differentiation, herd, and the protection found within numbers; that became the group, clan, and then the tribe. Separate, having their own identity, these groups of people repulsed any that were not within or of their own. Close-knit, the integrity and workability of the group depended on each member knowing or being told their place and part. Repulse kept one group or tribe separate from another. Separation bore the negatives so easily recognized today: hate, greed, avarice, harmfulness, pride, envy, anger, frustration and fear. All of these grow out of the recognition of who I am and that you are someone different, that I have or am capable of certain things and that you have or are capable of things often different from me and mine. By the Law of Attraction I desire to know, to feel, to be and incorporate into my experience all that is available, including that which is not mine. Repulse now is the attitude of the divine soul as it watches from a distance the grasping, wandering life of its reflection, the persona.

Separation also engendered positive results such as the value of the individual to the whole, and routinization and formalization that grew into distinct cultures and traditions. These kept the group unit coherent. Groups required land for sustenance and shelter. Tribes became nations, their habits became their individual national presence. Usually separate, often fighting one another, these groups continued until recent history to see separation and separate identity as the goal of life. Separate and unequal has worked the wondrous magic of creating a colorful, vibrant tapestry of experience for all members of the human race at every level of awareness. Repulse has kept humanity compartmentalized, stratified, and *class*-ified. As a result, art, philosophy, and inventions have sprung from individuals touched by the thoughts of people in other countries and centuries, as well as other traditions and beliefs.

Economics crossed the lines of demarcation creating new rings-pass-not where interchange took place; not just an interchange of commerce and monies but of ideas and philosophies as well. Now beginning to see and understand, humanity longed for more open sharing and less conflict. Repulse now was engaged in a different activity. Separation could be seen as the walls and veils that it creates, or that we create for ourselves. Through the sharing of philosophy and cultures, humanity could see that there is much more in common than had long been apparent to the eye.

The dissenters spoke a new language, one of the individual vision, with the individual appreciation of the self apart from the whole. The entrenched models of society were seen as stagnant, lacking vitality, and further, inappropriate for the individual's growth. Artists painted a new mural of cooperative interaction between deity and humanity and between man and man. The Renaissance, that led to the so-called Age of Enlightenment, gave us the freedom of thought, action, and desire we have today. It was a time of tremendous repulse, so much more than a time of attraction. Consider the scientific inquiry, populace uprisings, and the ceaseless and often inspired debates in universities and the Church.

Humanity still has wars of tribal integrity and national expression. Eastern Europe is a crying voice of pain, injustice, and dissolution. The Middle East, once the crossroads of the world and enriched by the exchange of cultures and ideas, is a point of tremendous tension. The lesser aspects of repulse, wielded by the personal self, will after much pain and suffering give way to the greater soul aspects of repulse. Truthful identity, that is not pigeon-holed into nationalities or traditions, is identity with and of soul. As individuals and their groups glimpse that truthful identity repulse is again actively engaged, this time with the soul's participation and direction. All that is not of the design and defined program of the soul is repulsed. Now incarnation upon incarnation is used as the garden in which the soul prunes and weeds, nurtures and reaps.

Pruning, the soul creates environments where right emotional response is cultivated. The person over time feels repulsed by their own reactiveness and lack of emotional control. Co-workers and family members are often repulsed by the person who is emotionally engaged, and eventually a need for rhythm is recognized. Slowly, right emotional response grows out of the discipline applied by soul, through cyclic and usually unnoticed impression, and by the personal self who feels this as a positive step. It might be totally for personal gain, but little by little the person curtails their harmful emotions and nurtures the more loving and giving ones. Wholesome emotions are kept and expanded and aggressive or self-destructive ones are defined, analyzed and transmuted. Changed and vibrationally enhanced, the astral/emotional vehicle grows strong and true to the note of soul. Pruned like a grape vine so that the main stem remains and not a plethora of wayward tendrils, the astral sheath becomes fruitful in its ability to relate harmoniously. The out-bursting tendrils that so easily became engaged no longer exist. Loving radiance and balanced emotional expression now define the astral vehicle.

Soul also weeds the over-grown mental vehicle. So much information, wrong thought, and illusion has taken root in the mind that the person has become separated from the wholeness of humanity and soul. Able to think, but too easily swayed by the thoughts of others or by erroneous thoughts by and of himself, the person's reality is constricted. Like a weed that chokes out a beautiful flower, the mind needs proper attention.

Attention is the key. With pulses of thought, the soul now attempts to reach the cluttered over-active mind. The pulses are full but still, in stark contrast to the random, scattered, but sometimes meaningful patterns in the mind. Attention is drawn to these soul pulses. Intrigued, inspired, and desirous of more, the person begins to recognize that only when the activity of the mind is altered can these pulses seep through. He can see the harmfulness of some of his thoughts to himself and others. Definition of the real and the illusory begins. Traps are revealed. Insight takes place.

One by one, thoughts and processes of thought that were brought together over a lifetime (and more) are looked at. Right discrimination determines the ones that are appropriate and life enhancing. Those that are false, destructive, or inappropriate are repulsed. The result is clarity and understanding. Thought forms are redeemed; mind patterns become thoughtful and not simply exercises in mental gymnastics. The mind, the slayer of the real for so long, has been weeded and cleaned of its clutter. The real, the beautiful, and the true can now make lasting impression upon the mental vehicle. And it, true to its design and because of repulse, can receive and begin to interpret those impressions.

Differentiation and repulse are the tools used by soul to split apart the emotion/mind (kama-manas[42]) that is the state of consciousness of most people. The masses of humanity dwell in a continuum of reactive relating because there is not yet the evolution of real independent and succinct thought. Usually good natured, well-intentioned, and seeking security, the masses approach life through the gratification of needs. Emotions create thoughts, thoughts bear emotions. The two are never separate. These two vehicles have their distinct vibrations but their rates are not far apart. Repulse has not occurred sufficiently to create a clear demarcation and subsequent enhancement that will release each vehicle into its own theater of operations and release the person onto the path of coordination. It is repulse that at some point takes hold and separates the two parts into two

---

[42] Kama-manas is Sanskrit. Literally translated kama – desire or feeling, manas – mind, therefore feeling mind.

wholes, distinct and apparent. From there the personality uses each in cultivating herself; then soul uses each through coordination and infusion to cultivate a conscious presence here on earth.

The masses are actively, though unconsciously, using repulse right now. On the physical level we see repulse of the tendency toward sloth and lethargy, that grew out of the leisure time available to many in the Western industrialized world. Many now walk or are involved a wide range of exercise regimes, recreational sport activities, and explorations into various methods of artistic creativity. Granted, these strenuous economic times find many having less time for leisure, as two incomes per household are common, as well as the family responsibilities. But here again repulse is the tool to prioritizing the precious time available.

Information about food and the clear medical linkage between healthier eating habits and a healthier, happier person have made many people in the industrialized world evaluate the quality of what goes into their body. The under-developed and less affluent countries still eat close to the land and therefore in a basically more healthful way. Where there is difficulty in growing or obtaining food, however, the situation is obviously very unhealthy. Slowly the masses are looking at how their food is grown, cooked, packaged, and discarded. Change is incremental and old habits hard to change. The masses in the United States still eat basically unhealthily and are being told so more and more by medical advisors.

As the masses look at the factor of food, they are looking at the pesticides that were used to grow that food, the children and migrant workers used to pick that food, the unsafe conditions in the factories that processed the food, and the multi-layered, big profit margin packaging in which that food was distributed. As the masses make the simple decision about what goes into their bodies they also decide what goes into the earth's body. Through repulse the masses are beginning to make choices for the better and the needs left un-addressed are made plain. Yet repulse is incremental and uses the gifts that time has to offer. Repulse done quickly is often not lasting repulse, but repulse done slowly, measuredly, makes for habitual change.

Emotionally, women are seeking independence. They are looking for validation for their emotional responses as well as a little distance from them, because with distance they are not swept away by their feelings. Men are trying to acknowledge and thereby grow more in sensitivity. They recognize that this is a valid part of oneself and in order to be whole this part must find its place and use. As a result boys are given more room to express how they feel. The process has only just begun and still many men, women, and children live in and are brought up in the old emotionally oppressive ways. That development will lead to more repulse as emotional reactivity will increasingly be seen as usually inappropriate and equally unhealthful.

The masses are also beginning to look at stress and its origins, at fear and hate, and at needs like security, well-being, and contentment. The work begun on the mental level is newer than that on the astral. Thought forms are solidified and hard to break. Repulse will help humanity look at worry and why we do this, anxiety and its negative results, at fear and hate, and issues of security or well-being for the individual, his family, country, and the world. Repulse of the old separative tribal ideas and ways, though modernly appearing more civilized and sophisticated, will take generations to be complete. The seeds of repulse are beginning to sprout, and the soul of humanity is watering and nurturing these important seeds.

Clear connections to any of the Beatitudes seem lacking. There is however that point in time and in the individual's evolution when instead of hungering and thirsting for material gains of the world, the person begins to hunger and thirst for righteousness. Obviously at this point a member of the masses begins the path of conscious evolution. Now he has set himself to a particular task, and that task will change his awareness and life processes forever. Once he begins to hunger and thirst for something less outwardly tangible he will begin to release and repulse his indoctrination to the material worlds. Perspective begins to turn around, and as a result the small selfish life begins to evolve into a more meaningful one.

This leads him, unconsciously, to the first two means of Yoga, yama and nijama, and at the same time to the Eightfold Path of the Buddha.

Through the gentle, quiet impress of soul these become subtle disciplines or altruistic endeavors in the life. The harmlessness and truthfulness of yama are used through right thought and right speech. Dealing with the various desires of the flesh, emotions, and mind, the personality engages the rest of yama - abstinence from greed, avarice, and incontinence of the emotional waters. But true yama, like true right thought, is not merely abstinence; it is the repulse of that which is not healthy to the body, emotions, or mind of the person or anyone else. This repulse is a clear decision based on information gathered through living experience and that to continue on as currently is to live a spiritually unhealthy life.

Nijama entails the external and internal purification associated with repulse. Clearly there are things that need to be left out or done away with in order to make room for a spiritually healthy existence. New habits need to be fostered, ones that allow for soul's presence to enter daily life. This presence inspires, uplifts and gives strength to endure the changes necessary during one's spiritual revolution. Through fiery aspiration and devotion (contained within nijama) the person employs right effort and is rewarded as soul's presence is felt more frequently and easily. This leads to contentment (also part of nijama). This spans many lives. Often extreme at first, then settling into a more moderate pace, the repulse of the unreal and unrefined exposes the real and the lighted; each half of the process fueling the other.

In time the wondering, questioning person grows into the insatiable aspirant desirous of all spiritual secrets and quick complete illumination. Again repulse is used by soul, training the aspirant in the cyclic seasons of work/rest, revelation/assimilation, and meditative "dry times" that are rich and full of contact, merely of a different kind. The aspirant must learn to repulse glamorous ideas and expectations of a relationship with soul and, instead, live the moment of soul's relating. More pruning of the astral nature and more weeding of the mental takes place until the tested aspirant develops an attitude of patient soul reception. This attitude or asana is a source of strength, poise and composure, mental clarity and emotional stability. It is, at the same time, gentle and powerful, resolute and bending.

Eventually it becomes continuous. Then the aspirant is no longer an aspirant, she or he is a disciple.

For the disciple, repulse and attraction are like her two feet. She walks both simultaneously, engaging each as methods to desired ends. Certainly disciples make mistakes. They are human, still very much part of the three worlds and as such give one aspect of life or living more emphasis than another. Here again soul employs repulse bringing definition to the purpose of any work undertaken. Repulse is used to clarify the details that need to be addressed and those of less importance. The result is a sense of priority, an unmistakable quality of a disciple. A better use of energy, as well as a well-spent employment of time become necessary as the disciple takes on more responsibility. Service and repulse, at this point on the path, meld into one activity. The disciple is capable of far-reaching work, work that the aspirant was unaware of and unready for.

As we approach the end of the Piscean Age that which was built but did not meet the full expectations of soul must be repulsed. The disciples within the body of humanity will actively take on this role. As examples, the single method of teaching - teacher to student, the strenuous endeavor to become an individual recognized for one's uniqueness, and a focus on the part thus not seeing the whole, must begin to be repulsed. As the student comes to appreciate the teacher in all forms of life and all circumstances in which he finds himself, then he will recognize the teachings at every hand, free for the taking and learning. The repulse of devotion to one teacher replaced by dedication to the One in all is a monumental step in the reorientation of the disciple. This has a rippling affect through all thought forms where one person is singled out and placed in lofty regard.

The need to be recognized as an individual led humanity to the point where it stands today, separate. Yet as with all steps along the way, this cycle was of paramount importance in the evolution of the person and society. As a result of the refinement of uniqueness and individual attributes, the single person's place within a group can now proceed. Humanity can step into the next phase of realization - group interaction. The ways of the individual for the sake of separate identity will be transformed and the ways of integral relatedness will be followed. In time, the uniqueness of the individual will stand more clearly revealed as the context of the group and group activity will allow the radiant shining of the evolved self.

For the disciple, The Angel with the Flaming Sword (the symbol of this law) intermittently comes into conscious play. He is dedicated to repulsing that which holds him down or back from constant contact with soul and from the understandings that will result. Portals of radiant ambiance appear in the disciple's meditation. New energy schemes stand behind see-through doors; words are almost heard reaching out from a wall of light. The disciple would enter into these heightened spaces unaware of the possible dangers to his energy system, his mind, and the balance for which he has long striven. He would pass through the door not realizing the responsibility inherent in that passing. If unaware of the danger and the responsibility then he or she is not ready to pass. Until the whole vibration of the soul-infusing personality is up to par with the revelation, the Angel will bar the way protecting what is within the disciple yet to be transformed and that which lies on the other side of the portal of consciousness. Often not seen as an angel or deva, but instead experienced as a question either by the Self or to the self, the disciple is stopped in thought. The temporarily accelerated vibration achieved by the disciple thus revealing the hidden door, decreases and the momentarily revealed is veiled again. The disciple and the profound are safe from premature exposure.

The Angel carries the flaming sword and wields it decisively; that which is not of soul and soul's determined course is stricken and slain. The Angel's power is that of the first ray (will and power) used by a second ray being (love and wisdom). The Angel knows the beneficent results of cleavage and removal. A glamour or illusion cut in half is half as strong, half as tempting. Granted there are now two where there once was one, but the two require less energy to dissipate. In the process of cleavage the old as well as the possible new are revealed. The strike of the Angel's sword is like a lightning bolt. It destroys, but it also illumines. The disciple gains perspective in the fleeting light of insight. He sees the pieces of himself that kept him from being whole. Now he can take the sword and work repulse in a new way.

With a touch of the sword, symbolizing his determination to tread the path of initiation, anything that is not refined is cut away. Essence and presence, power and wisdom radiate clearer, stronger. His heightened sense of love repulses the thoughts of being better or more advanced than his brother or sister, those thoughts now relegated to the separatism of the past. He does not repulse work in the three worlds, but instead knows it to be his duty, his dharma. He does not repulse matter, but instead engages matter, redefining it and thereby redeeming it. Now he can enter through the door and into the holy place of the mysteries. He can understand and recognize the responsibility that will be his when he leaves.

Through the path of discipleship and through the first few initiations, the Eightfold Path is walked increasingly until it becomes the very ground trodden.

The Eight Means of Raja Yoga are a linear progression in repulse, each means being determined by the repulse of the previous. The possibilities of nijama would be next to nil if yama were not first explored. Contentment easily flows as harmlessness is lived and the astral waters controlled. Fiery aspiration follow truthfulness to self and other. Devotion to the soul in all – Ishvara – is possible only when we see another as the soul and not just a source of things we want. The cycles of in-coming and out-going, in all dimensions and categories are most easily recognized from a poised position and an equally positive and receptive attitude. Thus pranayama can be known after asana is established. Attention or dharana has no meaning until after withdrawal and the subsequent quietude of pratyahara. And we cannot even consider the true meaning of dhyana – meditation - until after we have become as attentive to the subtle as we are to the concrete and the mundane. The activities of the mind, the turbulence of the emotions, and the desire for recognition of the personality must all be repulsed; simultaneously are they refined. Then after all these means to yoga are lived, refined, and re-defined can the disciple approach the most sublime act of repulse, samadhi. In repulsing all that is not of spirit, the yogi is identified as spirit. Once again we see that the sword of cleavage can bear exquisite results.

For the disciple the fields of repulse grow bigger and bigger. Refining all aspects of the personality until the fourth initiation[43], the disciple is ever turning the bend in the road and facing himself. More and more that face takes on the contours of the rest of humanity, the various kingdoms, and the soul. The more repulse, the more refinement; the more refinement, the more repulse, and essence. Thus the more essential the disciple's being becomes the more he engages life. Repulse now is the clear doing and being of his purpose. Via repulse he finds his group, his subjective and objective work, and the avenues for manifesting that work. It cannot be attraction that leads him to these doors. Attraction pulls equally in all directions and this same force would pull the disciple in many directions simultaneously, taking little recognition of his enhanced and useable qualities. But repulse more than notices these qualities - it is built on them. Repulse defines the vibration of the group that resonates in like manner to the disciple. Repulse pushes the disciple away from that which is not his to do while equally revealing his group and his work.

Like the stars and the planets held in their place in space by repulse, the groups around the world are held in designed spatial relationships. Through repulse their activities are enhanced and kept whole. Through repulse the integrity and uniqueness of each aspect of the work is maintained. The vibration or pulse reverberates like a beacon to the pulse and vibration within the disciple. Here is where repulse and attraction become almost one. Again that which is the tool of separation becomes the architect of inclusion.

The disciple has come around to being "the pure in heart" of the Beatitudes. The kingdom of heaven stands revealed within her and all around her. She can see the designs made possible by repulse and set by the Creator for all to see. She has learned mercy through the process of repulse and so stands as the "merciful". Mercy flows out of contentment. At first, contentment seemed far removed from the disciple attached to what was being repulsed, but as soul design could be seen and as the life took on rhythm

---

[43] The fourth initiation called in the East, Renunciation, in the West, Crucifixion. This is the initiation of liberation from the three worlds of human attachments. With this initiation one becomes a "true soul" free to serve in the three worlds unfettered or to serve from the kingdom of souls and stay dis-carnate.

and purpose, contentment was felt. Contentment became a part of the act of repulse. Repulse became the totally positive activity that it is. Mercy and understanding now flowed from the soul into and through the soul-infusing disciple.

The initiates stand free having repulsed all that is not designed by the divine. They have *entered* the designs and from this position their soul-fullness and refined integrity speaks. Initiates identify their specific work, likewise the work of their brothers and sisters, by the delineation of their energies. In this way the work is done most efficiently. Networking and partnership are entered knowing fully the qualities to be used and employed. Failure to accomplish the desired ends would be next to impossible.

The initiates must bring the work into manifested form, even if the form is in the realm of thought or feeling. Now humanity becomes part of the work and with that the increased possibility of a less than perfect outcome. The reason for this is that most people are not aware of their own energies or those around them; also they have not identified the many layers in which their energies move or the effects of them. On the other hand, the initiates are aware of their energies and their effects thus not only do they use theirs with agility but all energies available to them.

Initiates have achieved unity with the Whole. Their vibration has grown strong and exquisite. Like beacons they shine. Using the dual process of attraction/repulsion they create a whole – a project, an endeavor, an ashram - vibrating to their note and in sync with the design of God. The individual note of each initiate (third degree or above) hums attractive and magnetic on the inner planes. Its vibration goes out and attracts those similarly resonating. Those who are not of this vibration will find another and another work of service in the world. The magnetic warmth and loving understanding that exudes from initiates of high degree will be felt by all (as peace, compassion, presence, power), but the pull to do work affiliated with that particular individual, endeavor, or ashram, will not be there.

One cannot enter the temple of the soul or its kingdom unless one has sanctified one's existence. Repulse is never-ceasing, like the work of soul. Repulse is an avenue to joy, as well as the road to essence and beyond.

The Eightfold Path and The Eight Means to Yoga have lead the disciple to the various doors of renunciation and repulse, and because of those doors the disciple is made whole and initiate. The particular Beatitudes that convey the meanings of integrity, completeness, purity, and divine understanding will always apply to the initiates. They are the realized and therefore bestow realization.

The fourth law of the soul, The Law of Repulse, has correlation to six out of seven systemic laws. To the Law of Vibration, because repulse is the enhancement and refinement of vibration. In this way atoms are defined, as well as solar systems. By vibration all life is known and made tangible. Vibration is what denotes quality energetically, therefore, it is vibration that determines a ray from a ray, a strong force from a weak force, a wave from a particle.

To the Law of Cohesion, for as consciousness seeks to incarnate, in form large or small, repulse is the tool of corporeal intactness. Via repulse cohesion is made easier. Basically that which is of use is used, and that which is not is rejected. This is fairly easy to see in the three lower kingdoms. A rock, mountain, steel girder, or wedding ring stays intact until natural processes undo its coherency and the law of disintegration takes over. An animal chooses the stuff to construct its den, nest, or hive. It lasts at least one season, more often for years. In the human kingdom, however, we see many struggling through their daily lives with matters seemingly not of soul's design. The reason for this is that the human soul is not perfected and therefore will draw to itself that which also is not perfected. In this regard we look to karma as well. Karma is like glue, that which was set in motion a moment ago, or any other lifetime ago, adheres to us until we are conscious enough to undo it. Coherence is integrity. Integrity is a result of repulse.

The Law of Magnetic Control designates the manner in which the personality will be refined and therefore vibrate to the soul's required frequency. Magnetically the soul draws the attention of personality. Controlling factors, such as personality interest in the ways of spirit, effort, aspiration, discipline, and attitude determine the speed or lack thereof in the controlling process. Repulse and love are the primary methods of control.

But of all the systemic laws it is the Law of Fixation that has the most correspondence with the Law of Repulse. Fixation is delineation employing the mental processes of definition and determination. Fixation is the establishment of right order through correcting that which was not in rhythm with the fundamental plan of soul and spirit. Establishing the parameters, fulfilling those requirements, and making firm and lasting the desired result is fixation. Stability is the effect of the Law of Fixation both upon the mind, its main target, and the life. Stability also is the result of repulse. The essential is all that remains after the long cyclic work of repulse between personality and soul, and then soul and monad.

Soul is fixed in space. Its presence is concrete. It has dimension and influence. That influence has a ring-pass-not described and enhanced by repulse. At some point in time (in which soul is not fixed hence phrases like "the eternal now") soul will repulse even its spatial existence. The causal body[44] will disintegrate and conscious identity and essence will be absorbed back into monad that now has a refined, spiritualized personality with which to touch the worlds.

Monad is fixed in time. Eternal and eternally involved in the materialization of Itself, monad is time. We live because monad chose to breathe. Its breath will last a particular duration and then we will not be, and yet we will, because we are part of that timely breathing process. Monad is now, present, and presence. Monad is power; and time is power. Time is, for spatial entities like us, the greatest ring-pass-not. Time is discipline. Time is revolution. Time cannot be escaped. It cannot even be bent. We can only bend to its over-arching unremittance. Only monad has the power of time because that is its fixity. Time is a measure of monad's design and a hint of its purpose.

Through the Law of Love we learn discretion. The differences between desires, wants, and true needs are made abundantly clear. Distance is gained resulting in detachment. Passions are understood and compassion, Love, is enhanced.

---

[44] The causal body is the body of the soul itself. Synonymous terms are: the Temple of Solomon, the Golden Bowl, the egoic lotus.

The Law of Sacrifice and Death negates that which is of the will of the personality and the self-consciousness of any of the vehicles. Self-will is seen for its limitations. The will of the soul would include the smaller wills if they would reorient their focus and no longer seek the ways of separation. In sacrifice that is their death, the smaller (at any level of consciousness or in any form) become part of the greater; likewise their wills are released into a greater expression of self-hood.

In other words, as The Law of Repulse interacts with these systemic laws these results are evident:

Systemic Law	**Result**
Vibration	Enhancement
Cohesion	Integrity
Magnetic Control	Definition
Fixation	Design
Love	Dispassion
Sacrifice/Death	Free Will

Figure 19

The cosmic Law of Attraction in many ways seems to be the polar opposite of the Law of Repulse, yet the two are inextricably linked. The yin and yang of the creative process or more accurately the appropriator of matter and the tools of design, attraction and repulse cannot be without each other. Both employ the word or resonating sound to achieve their purposes. Both require the honest vision of the whole essential self. Both require significant time.

The First Ray of Will or Power and The Law of Repulse

The First Ray is the ray of "beneficent destruction." It is power, essence, and reality. The first ray is not stopped by the details of life because it sees life in its widest exposure and fullest expression. In so doing, detail is included but not given extra emphasis. However, the Law of Repulse works only with detail, with the refining process, and in the end even refines the process itself. This it does so that only the essence or consciousness remains, then on a higher turn the spirit.

Repulse reveals definition. It makes contours and veiled images appear, as the background is negated and gossamer sheaths removed. Light and dark are left naked, there for all to see, even if the only one noticing is the disciple himself. At first hurt, assailed, and thrown back, the disciple feels violated. The first ray deals little with pretext. It hurts. It heals. The first ray reveals in flashes of lightning and reduces things to nakedness. One cannot retreat, like one cannot retreat from repulse.

Many people are repulsed by the power and willfulness of the untempered first ray. Without love and kindness, it destroys all within its path. Yet the Law of Repulse is a law of love because it is a law of the soul. Love is its very motivation and purpose; inclusion its denouement.

The first ray of Will and Power would seem merciless, yet mercy is a virtue of the spirit expression of this ray, as is harmlessness and a commanding knowledge of all the details, yet detachment from their clinging intricacies. Generating electric vibrations into all aspects of the self, the soul uses its power to isolate the real and the unreal, a process painful to the shadow self. Once revealed it can no longer be hidden, and certainly not swept back under the rug. It must be dealt with.

The first ray deals with things, forthrightly, absolutely, completely. It leads the personality in the strength of soul, with the commitment of aspiration, in order to endure the hardship. Fearless and courageous, the first ray takes action. The sword cuts through, the self bleeds. Repulse is decisive action eventually done with mercy and always with the love of soul. That is its power and its truth.

Repulse reveals design. The designed intention of the first ray is symbolized by both the straight line and the dot. Nothing on either side, nothing surrounding it, the first ray is isolated in essential being. Repulse isolates, stripping away the insulation that has deadened sensory acuity to the real. Pure first ray reveals all that is unreal and all presentations or manifestations in life that are only partial. Spirit is totality, and first ray is related spirit, its breath, and the breadth of life. Then in the absolute (or first ray) sense, everything is unreal, a reflection or part of the whole.

The first ray evokes response, yet it stands whole and unperturbed by that which is evoked. This is repulse and must happen. The personal response to it is far less important than the repulse itself. Repulse sets many things in motion, as does the first ray.

The First Ray of Will or Power

Will	creates	Direction
Power	is	Dynamism
Breath of Life	is	Electric Light
Destroyer/Death	leads to	Liberation/Freedom
Complete within the Self	brings	Synthesis
Purpose	is	Intended Totality

Figure 20

Repulse leads to integrity on all levels. This also is a first ray virtue, though rarely seen in human beings because of their personal lack of purity, thus the negative power, will, domineering side of this ray is what manifests. This ray is, though, the ray of pure power, pure light, pure law, pure synthesis - One. Fully expressed, the first ray is complete negation of all that is separative. It is the breath of Life itself.

Repulse leaves us only with the breath, the vibrating word, intoning in space rhythmically in time. Mercifully the Angel with the Flaming Sword separates us from the real and the unreal, making the difference between the darkness and the light quite clear. The first ray is death and immortality. Aspects of the self must die in order to give expression to the fullness of Self.

The masses are afraid of repulse. They fear its lack of sentimentality. Personally they wish for less clarity and less directness. Repulse could seem indiscriminate at this level, and yet is so precise. It is like a hammer and chisel in the hands of a great sculptor. He sees the quality hidden within the block of marble. The artist works painstakingly, tirelessly, fearlessly, chipping away the grossness, until finally with intricate precision, he approaches the subtlety hidden within the rock. The beauty of the essence can be seen.

The First Ray of Will or Power and the Masses

Will	leads to	Willfulness
Power	leads to	Power hungry/ wrong use of power
Strength	leads to	Control
Fearlessness	leads to	Ambition
Independence	leads to	Self-serving

Figure 21

Disciples invite repulse, begrudgingly at first, then graciously. As soul and spirit are glimpsed more frequently, and as rhythm and tension are felt in life's experience, the disciple begins to know the worth of this process. He stands strong, even to a certain extent fearless. He has courage to endure the endless path of repulse he is on. He feels isolated, though, as most of the people around him do not invite the sword of repulse not seeing the possible good that will result. Yet the feelings of unity get stronger with each detachment. Repulse begins to seem actually quite beneficial, an interesting mystery to the disciple.

The First Ray of Will or Power and Disciples

Courage	creates	Truthfulness
Essence oriented	brings	Understanding the big picture
Purposeful	means	Direct in thought and action
Detached	is to be	Able to destroy the old; new can take its place
Power used for the greater good	is	Moving from the center out to the goal

Figure 22

Initiates only work with essence, so repulse is ever engaged. The first ray position of commander is theirs, not over any one person, but in command of the energies at hand. Refined and distinct, the work to be undertaken is done wholly with all their presence. They are the Sword of God and the Embodiment of the Mysteries.

The First Ray of Will or Power and the Initiates

Law	is	To wield energy and light
Power of Love	is	The Greatest Power
Identity	knows	Life is One
Will	is	Singleness of Purpose
"When thine eye is single"	then	"All is Light"

Figure 23

The Chakras, Vehicles, and The Law of Repulse

The chakras are spinning vortices of force with their rate of spin correspondent to the force flowing through them. Their vibration corresponds to the plane of being the chakra is allied to. Symbols that can be seen clairvoyantly in or around the chakras refer to many things including the rays that pour through them. These rays change as the person evolves and re-defines his internal energetic structures. The chakras are distinct, separate, functioning distinctly and separately. All these things are an aspect of repulse.

Repulse maintains spatial placement within the chakric system. It creates the boundaries or rings-pass-not around each center. Each chakra vibrates to its own particular rate, thus repulsing anything that is not of a similar rate, as seen with all other forms of life, great and small. The repulsing action is part of what creates the etheric web that separates the chakras. The web is a physical manifestation of repulse in action.

For vast periods of time the chakras work primarily in one direction – inward - extracting subtle energies from experience and thus helping to build the subtle vehicles (etheric aura, emotional/astral body, mental body). Like tiny black holes, they absorb all that comes their way that is of similar essential quality. The chakras open into the planes of corresponding matter, (etheric, astral, mental) depositing the newly sucked in matter. This is one part of the process that grows the vehicles.

Once a vehicle has developed a modicum of definition and is full of this first type of matter, the chakras related to this vehicle begins to take on a second motion. Previously, the chakra was like a funnel that opened into an open space. Anything flowing through the funnel was deposited into the relatively defined cavern of the vehicle. Now the clutter and fullness of the cavern, or vehicle, requires a release and a cleaning out. The inside end of the funnel (chakra) begins to turn outwardly. It spins and draws from inside all that is unnecessary, undefined, unrefined, or inappropriate to the point of vibration and quality at which the vehicle now stands. The vehicle has begun to incorporate itself, to have minimal integrity, and recognizes that much of what it has acquired is of no use.

The chakra takes on a dual function and a two-fold action. Still it spins inwardly and draws on the experiences of life for the sustenance and growth of the vehicles and the consciousness. It also, but not equally, spins from the inside to out, repulsing, releasing, defining the vehicles, their parameters, and their intactness. The vibration of both the vehicle and the chakra accelerate and are enhanced. This point is where most of humanity is today with fairly established vehicles in dire need of definition and clarity.

As the chakras throw off that which is negative or unusable, light results. The vehicle, in time, grows lighter in density and luminosity. The chakra now takes on vibrancy, as two forms of fire are in use: fire by friction and the solar fire of consciousness. Fire by friction is evident in the dual activity of the chakra and in the throwing off process. The fire of consciousness is three-fold. The chakra itself, in performing a major part of its designed and elevated function, becomes aware of that which passes through it. It learns of the matters of the corresponding vehicle. Previously, there was no cognition, only absorption. Now there is intelligence and a degree of consciousness. Secondly, the vehicle is aware of its process and engages the chakra more knowingly. And thirdly, that which is passed through in both directions is also refined or minimally changed by the sheer exchange of energies and the use of the fires. Through the process mini veils are removed and more quality is expressed.

This light, this vibrancy, is radiation. The chakra begins to radiate. The vehicle begins to radiate. The radiance further expresses both, and the personality is on its way to fulfillment. Radiance is ever a sign of integrity and once a vehicle has integrity it can then be coordinated with the other vehicles and integrated. Following that, it can be infused with soul light.

Chakras now begin to express something of their design, their greater purpose. They can be seen as the great conductors of force and the great transmuters of quality that they are. Through repulse and subsequent refinement, the chakras become purified and all that passes through them from the outer worlds is also refined.

Refinement and transmutation become interwoven accomplishments. The chakra throws off the lesser and becomes rarified. The forces used in and by the chakra also become rarified. Now the energies of the sacral center, for instance, vibrate to a rhythm that is similar to and supported by the throat center. By attraction and magnetic impulse the lower center's energies are pulled up and more transmutation occurs. Eventually this energy returns and the sacral center, completely redeemed, vibrating to its intended design. It now can draw upon a completely different ray energy than it did for centuries, if not millennia. It spins in two directions simultaneously, and so takes on a third mode of activity.

Only repulse could allow for such seemingly impossible physical feats. The already three dimensional chakra now becomes fourth dimensional. In and out, up and down, around and through, completely centered, isolated and coordinated, spiraling in time, the chakra's design is revealed. The chakra is one of the purest instruments used to materialize spirit and spiritualize matter.

Attraction and repulse again become the two sides of a same-headed coin. That which separated also refined, and that which was refined sang out its song of attraction and invitation. Matter of all levels can be attracted but then must undergo the strenuous ordeal of repulse and of definition. In being defined all parts know their place. In knowing their place they become a useable and intelligent part of the design. In becoming the design, whole schemes of life are expressed and thereby experienced. That creates the need for more definition and clearer understanding of the design. On and on, finer and finer, repulse after repulse; until complete revelation.

Chapter Six

The Fifth Law of the Soul
The Law of Group Progress
The Law of Elevation

From this point forward we speak little of the masses except that they are moved by ideas translated through those of wider consciousness. As the last three laws of the soul are lived they require that the individual be aligned, aware, decreasing the ego and distributing the light of life into the realms of form. The means to yoga, the Beatitudes, and the eight of the Noble Middle Path likewise will not be singled out. We will not speak of chakras, for the disciple-initiate is a chakra within the human kingdom, that is to say, that person has become a focal point of particular work, related to and using a particular chakric focus, and will leave a legacy that will be distinctly related to and tell-tale of the materialization of divine intent.

In order to see expressions of the Fifth, Sixth, and Seventh Laws of the Soul we will use the eye of insight because these laws pertain more to the form sublime than to the outer form. With them we enter the heights of conscious understanding and the subtle manifestations of soul. Examples will be given that one might say are quite external and manifested, but the expressed form is only evidence that the law is lived. The inner relation to the law is what we seek to illumine.

It is with the Law of Group Progress that one of the most primary forms in existence makes its mark. It is so concrete that pyramids are based upon it, atoms are three-fold because of it, and the Trinity or Triplicity of Deity is its progenitor. This form is the triangle. And with it the use of "soul geometry" and the "science of triangles" find their perfected use.

There is a difference between the word group used esoterically and the common thought of being in a group. Occultly, group is only possible once soul is part of the habitual functioning of the person. To be in a group and to participate in the activities of a group does not necessitate that. Fraternities, organizations, clubs, cliques are a normal part of our everyday world. In these examples the personalities are quite involved, and possibly the only thing that is. Group, group awareness and functioning is unhindered by personality, time, place, or proximity. It is a method employed, a technique used, and a dynamic aspect of being aligned with spirit, the spirit in all of life.

What does group mean? Group is a state of consciousness born of the soul thus producing the activities required by spirit.

Group is that point of selflessness where all selves are blended into one Self. All minds share the thought processes. All love and compassion are directed toward a common goal, and all activities are coordinated into a coherent single functioning. Each knows the part and function of the others. Indeed, each part creates the greatest functioning of the other parts. Each is equally important, none more or less so. A profound equanimity pervades this point of selflessness. This is why and how it works so well, and how progress is attained. The progress has little to do with the personal, but is instead the progress achieved of some part of the Plan, large or small.

Group is a level of soul identification with the purpose of the Monad, where there is only one point of reference and that is the spirit and its needs. All individuals are at one with that need. There is nothing else to do or be part of. All move in the right flow with one another, like a school of fish sensing the movement of the sea currents. Little energy is wasted or time lost as the fullness of potential works out.

We could wonder why this is the fifth law. Think of the tremendous work of decentralization established via the other four laws. Consider the increased identification with and of soul that has been nurtured and groomed. With Sacrifice we learned of our wants, desires, and needs. We learned to move away from the small focus of the personal and move to the larger focus of others, sacrificing our own so that others might be freer. With Magnetic Impulse we found ourselves being attracted to others who helped us learn soul lessons. Karma played out, and though pain was a part of the process, we were changed, uplifted and altered, as were they. With Service we experimented with ourselves, how to give, where to help, and why we were moved to do so. We began to see our glamours about service, our needs to serve, to fix, to set things right. And with Repulse we began to eject that which no longer served the whole of our being. We learned proper discrimination and began it with ourselves. We learned detachment and how to lift our eyes up off the personal self.

These four laws enabled the soul to take firm hold of the personality and mold it into a workable, useful instrument. The personality has recognized the process and has pledged to get out of the way of the light of soul and to be in line with the intentions of spirit. Sacrifice has taken the form of a pledge of aspiration and dedication.

Through Repulse the disciple learned to define and delineate that which served him well and that which now could be discarded. Repulse taught him to assess energies, forces, and vibrations and to be aware of how they move ceaselessly within and around him. Now the Law of Group Progress could begin to move into his life. Having learned discrimination he can tell the difference between energy and force, between that which he is and that which is other. Discrimination and analysis have given the disciple the tools to be a knowledgeable worker in the Divine Plan. But more than understanding energies and focal points of actuated design, this disciple-initiate also has seen the vision of the completed result. He knows the instructions of how to be a part of the workings thus insuring that the work will be done correctly and occultly.

The Law of Group Progress is a law of co-measurement, co-operation, co-delineation, co-ordination, and of augmentation. In defining these terms we define the tools of Group Progress.

Co-measurement is the ability to move in direct response to the moment and all that is contained within that moment. Co-measurement is immediate, symmetrical, and correspondent. It is a method of right adjustment, never to much or too little. Discernment is the key because discrimination might tend to see only what is apparent whereas discernment is more subtle and recognizes that which is trying to work out. Discernment takes account of the probable and so anticipates future co-measurement.

Co-measurement is the synthetic discernment and analysis of what is around one and the ability to move with the least disruption of that continuum, yet also with the fullest expression of the potential pervading that continuum. In other words, the disciple-initiate is very aware of the qualities existent and expressing within an event or fellow person or co-worker, but is likewise cognizant of that which seeks fuller expression within the life or person. The initiate can quietly facilitate the working out of these more refined qualities by generating response from the other through co-measurement. Like begets like is a homeopathic truism. A quality demonstrated by one person tends to create a space that the other person fills with a similar vibratory quality. This process tends toward gentility and ease and works with the lines of least resistance between the two people and their inherent energies. As an example, courage or steadfastness lived by one person invite the same in another. Poise or decisive action expressed in someone draws forth the same in others.

Co-operation is the ability to act together, function together, and to operate literally by combining the gifts of each into a better whole. There is a give and take, a reciprocity with co-operation. Selflessness is constantly the point of view as is the resultant whole that is the work. Co-operation employs the emotions or heart and the mind by requiring precise action and the ability to move as others move.

Co-delineation starts with the ability to see the end before the first step towards it is taken. Lines of energy are drawn in the mind of God and in the minds of the co-workers. They see the lines along which they work, along which the work will proceed, and along which the Plan will manifest such as time lines, lines of energy progression, and lines of communication. These lines are activated and energized. It becomes obvious which ones will work well with each other, that are in resonance or enhance the employment or deployment of others. The responsibility is completely shared and co-delineation is established. Equally, the people are the points through which these lines of energy, quality, and manifestation pass. They are the terminal points. As such, co-measurement and co-operation are skillfully used so that cooperative delineation of all tasks results.

Co-ordination is about co-ordinates. These are the focal points in time and space for the lines to proceed, intersect, and be furthered through the addition of other qualities of energy. Literally the individuals become co-ordinates of energy specificity and condensations of forces to be manipulated. These co-ordinates create configurations of light and vibration. Geometrical patterns are produced with life giving and life changing energies flowing in specific ways through specific points. Triangles are the most basic and fundamental of these patterns and it is this law that governs all triangulation work. An example might be many people linking weekly in meditation focused on the right use of money in the world. Whenever and wherever they subjectively meet a network of light and consciousness is established and extended over the world. "Ask and it shall be given; seek and ye shall find" is an occult law. Therefore, as this net of meditative light is re-energized weekly, it grows more invocative and powerful. Slowly but surely men and women awaken to right use of money in their own lives.

Triangulation and Triangles

The disciple-initiate has arrived at a point of knowledge understanding the inherency, the use, and management of energy and force. This person knows what is alive within her, within others, and within the forms of life. But more importantly, she understands how those energies and qualities move with others. Like a painter, she has learned the fundamentals of blending colors together, and though not a master artist she can nonetheless create works of art and beauty. Through the years she will learn to work with facility and increased ease with others, thus will the beauty of the Plan in the Mind of God work out.

Triangulation is truly an art. Three notes make a chord. Each lends harmony to the other, but together they give us something that cannot be offered with less than three parts. It is the triplicity of the Trinity in expression. Triangles are created of the two foundational points and the apex. Three lines connect the coordinating points. When taken out of the limitations of two-dimensional space any one of the three points can be the beginning, middle or end or the foundational points and the apex. Each part is necessary to the other parts and no one point is more important than another. In order for the triangle to be whole all three points and the connecting lines are required. Likewise in triangulation of energies, each point of reference or distribution is as important as the other two. Whether the example is a chakric triangle, leigh lines of the earth, or three people in the world, the premise is the same. Each point augments the work of the whole. Each point sends the energy on to the next point slightly charged, changed, or enhanced by the former.

Triangles and triplicity are everywhere. Some examples are:

will	love	intelligence
spirit	consciousness	matter
life	quality	form
synthesis	attraction	economy
Shiva	Vishnu	Brahma
Father	Son	Holy Ghost
Om	Tat	Sat
Unmanifest Being	Great Spirit	Divine Mother
mental	emotional	physical
Monad	soul	personality
Atma	Buddhi	Manas
Higher Mind	Son of Mind	concrete mind
rajas (activity)	sattva (equilibrium)	tamas (inertia)
electric fire[45]	solar fire	fire by friction
sacrifice petals[46]	love petals	knowledge petal
pingala[47]	sushumna	ida

---

[45] The three fires of life are electric fire, solar fire, and fire by friction.
[46] The egoic lotus is a presentation of the soul and the evolution of human consciousness. It is the model upon which the chakras are based. It is comprised of three levels or tiers of petals, bottom – petals of knowledge or intelligence, middle tier – petals of love, and top tier – sacrifice or will petals. They unfold commensurate with consciousness.

Shamballa	Hierarchy	Humanity
judicial	legislative	executive
reading	writing	'rithmetic
mind	soul	brain
height	depth	width
cardinal cross[48]	fixed cross	mutable cross

Figure 24

Each of these triplicities or triangles relates to the three-foldness of Deity. In Hindu it is Shiva, Vishnu, Brahma. In Christian terms it is Father, Son, Holy Ghost. In occultism it is spirit, soul, form. And in Raja Yoga it is life, quality, and appearance.

The Law of Group Progress and triangulation require a refined knowledge of the subtle and the potentials that are as yet unseen. Knowledge is of different categories, born of different levels of mind apprehension. The plane of Manas, where mind is found, is itself triple in nature.

The concrete (lower) mind used by us all has knowledge of the tangible, the phenomenal worlds, and the form. The Son of Mind (soul) has knowledge of the subtle and the meanings behind the forms. And Abstract (higher) mind has knowledge of the purpose or intention that the meanings seek to convey. Higher mind is how we begin to know the Plan in the Mind of God. Through soul we begin to serve the Plan. Through the concrete mind we put our affairs in order so that the mundane world's concerns do not distract our focus from the greater work at hand.

The reason this is mentioned is because the fifth law of the soul utilizes "soul geometry." This is the "science of triangles." By looking at the various triplicities, the basic and correspondent three-foldness of life is easily seen. We begin to recognize that this three-foldness is a primary mechanism of the spiritualization of matter and the materialization of

---

[47] The three parts of the sutratma, that is the threefold thread of life that runs through the middle of the etheric body, upon which the seven primary chakras are found. Ida is the lunar or matter aspect, pingala is the solar or conscious aspect, sushumna is balance.

[48] The three crosses in astrology. Cardinal cross pertains to beginnings and the use of personal and spiritual will; fixed cross pertains to persistence, solidity, anchoring and manifesting; and the mutable cross pertains to flexibility and adaptability in mind, matter, emotions, truths, and visions.

spirit. Recognized is the fact that in the movement of energies and forces through the triangles formed of the three aspects of Life, all life takes shape, moves, and evolves. The Law of Group Progress decrees that there is a specific method of evolution, that it will almost infallibly bring about the desired results, and that the method is the science of triangles. The Seventh Ray, the major ray of this law, can be heard in these thoughts of specificity and organized use. There is order to the Universe, order to Life, and if we, or any other life form, seek to live in a greater measure of harmony with Life then we must recognize that harmony is order. This harmonic resolve is revealed through the triplicity of triangles and in the results of their use.

The Seventh Ray of Order, Organization, and Magic

All according to Divine Order	as seen through	Systems macro and micro
The Four (or Seven) Directions	bring	Orientation
The Temple	becomes	Foundations of Life
Spiritualization of Matter	leads to	Materialization of Spirit
Alchemy	is	Magic
Rhythm	is seen in	Timing and Progression
Patterns	create	Structure

Figure 25

The seventh ray gives us management, orchestration, and the right order and use of all parts. It also gives us organization via structures created of energetics and form. Literally with this law, the initiate is part of the structure of an energetic form. By it matter is instructed in ways of change from the inside out. There is appropriateness to it all, another seventh ray quality, in that matter of a particular nature is not asked to be something it cannot be. It is not stretched beyond its capabilities. This matter and these forms need to be used as tools of elevation. Likewise will the indwelling and coordinating consciousness be elevated.

Let us illustrate with an example of triangulation of energies. Within the human chakra system there are many potential triangles. In fact the number of working triangles is dependent upon where the person stands on the path of evolution. One triangle very common in most people is sacral, solar plexus, and throat. The sacral center is the place of our material desires and our security in the world. The solar plexus is a center of caring what people think of us, worry and anxiety. And the throat is the use of the concrete mind to get what we want through the use of words and manipulation. Each of these centers is much more than this example yet it easily illustrates a triangle alive, fully functioning and obvious in most people. On a higher turn of the spiral this same triangle would express very differently. The sacral center would be stability in matter and the desire to make concrete that which is touched in the spiritual realms. The solar plexus would be the center of allowing presence and commonalty. Through this center we truly care. And the throat would express words of wholeness, thoughts of the good, the true and the beautiful. Together these three would be wonderfully creative, invocative, and magnetically expressive. Our lives, cultures, and museums are filled with the gifts of people who had this chakric triangle alive within them. Theirs are the gifts of art, philosophy, science, theology, and the humanities.

The Seventh Ray of Order, Organization, and Magic and the masses

Order	leads to	Ordered living – rules and man-made laws
Routine	leads to	Habits in daily life
Coordination	creates	Being able to work with others (family, workplace)
Appropriateness	creates	Common decency and basic respect
Form bound (the letter of the law not the meaning or spirit)	creates	Customs, traditions, cultural biases
Importance of Appearance	leads to	Judgment based on the external; criticism
Superstition	leads to	Being seduced and held by phenomena

Figure 26

Energies are alive. Beings work en rapport with one another's inner radiance. Every component of a triangle is dynamic, vital, and vibrates its very essence. None of that is to be lost in or during the triangulation. Instead all parts are to be enhanced, each being revealed more through the process; likewise does the process create a living vitalizing and life enhancing mechanism.

In the Law of Repulse the idea of definition was conveyed. Definition is very specific, detailed and qualified. With the Law of Group Progress it is the idea of "specific" that underlies all workings.

The triangle is more than just a symbol of the triplicity of deity. It is the form that expresses and utilizes each of the three aspects of God. Within triangulation work each point represents or expresses one aspect primarily. Referring back to the chakric example, throat is aligned with will, solar plexus with love, and sacral with knowledge or matter. In World War II the three representatives of the Allied Powers were Churchill for England representing will, Roosevelt for the United States representing love, and Stalin for Russia representing the form. These positions are directly related to their inherent qualities and the rays are the simplest way to see that. England has a strong 1st ray, the U.S. the 2nd, and Russia the 7th. These three countries became the focal points for the liberation of humanity. All other allied countries were included in the work yet these three were the points through which the greatest down flow of energy happened. And it was interesting to observe nearly three decades later the same triangle was re-engaged in ending the Cold War.

Another good example of triangulation in the mundane is the United States system of government. The three branches of government again represent clearly the three aspects of deity in form. The legislative is supposed to be "for the people and by the people," though it usually falls far short of that. With wooing voters, and the needs of the constituency we can see the love aspect at work. The glamour of popularity and the inertia of trying to please many at once are of the love aspect and not the power or creative intelligent aspects.

One would see the word executive and automatically assume the 1st ray and therefore the will aspect of life. But in this form of government it is not necessarily so. The judicial branch holds the key to freedom in this country, not the executive. The president and all other officials are bound by the Constitution and the Laws of the Land. They cannot take all power into their hands but are bound by the edicts of Law set down through the short history of America. We can see how often the Law and the Supreme Court literally were the road to freedom. The ending of slavery, the right to vote for women, the civil rights movement, and the opportunities of the educational system regardless of race are just a few examples. Via the law, people have the right to impeach a leader, express themselves fully, and live as they choose. With freedom came the equal responsibility of living in a way conducive to all and not just to the selfish self. The United States as a nation is still learning that. But by and large the principles upon which the great laws are built are principles of freedom and the inherent equality of man.

It is interesting and important to note that the destroyer component of the will can also be seen through the law and the judicial branch. Manifest Destiny proceeded, trampling the Native Nations and the riches of their culture with the sanction of "white man's" laws. Treaties, supposedly legal and binding, were designed, discussed, and signed. Yet the liberation that they provided for some was the destruction of others.

The executive branch then becomes the means of enforcing and maintaining order and management of the country. Through the executive branch's need for order and stability bureaucracy, detail, agenda, regulations are created. These are far from liberating. Often they are stifling. The creative intelligence of Deity is reflected, though often poorly, in this branch of the government.

Triangles are the basic method of putting parts together thus affecting the whole. The effect will pervade all levels of life because with the triangle and the triplicity all levels have been involved. This leads us to the secondary name of this law, "the Law of Elevation." Force is elevated to the condition of energy. Energy is blended fully with quality. This unique blend ultimately brings equality to all the points within the triangle. Then the discrepancy that was the catalyst of the flow between points at the beginning no longer exists. Now the triangle is a unified, concurrent emanation of energy, purpose, and pure thought. As the energies flow the triangle loses its hard angles and edges and rounds itself out thus becoming a multi-dimensional circle.

Triangles are a vital part of the functioning of Hierarchy, the Kingdom of Souls. Work is constant between ashrams, masters, adepts and their groups of chelas. Groups are created out of the triangulation work, so that more than three people might eventually be involved in some business or energy interplay but it will always be found that three are the focal points of the design and purposeful activity of the group. They maintain the lines of the work. They stay attuned to the vision of the completed whole so that all parts remain true to the intention. They are the points of tension through which the greatest energy flows, energy being then immediately directed into the group and the group's field of endeavors.

Interestingly, triangles are not bound by ashramic affiliation but are the wise use of individuals for the greatest return of willed quality. Often people have had working relationships before, and having profited by them, a higher turn of the spiral can take place. Literally, energies and qualities are combined that will create the greatest result.

For another example of triangulation, we can look to the natal charts of people and see that the elements and the crosses relate certain qualities of force within our lives and in the movements with others throughout our lives. The understanding of these would reveal how soul (and Monad on a higher turn) chooses to elevate matter into spirit and immerse spirit into matter. Indeed, the reading of astrological charts is learning and understanding triangulation, not only the angles of the planets in their signs, but the orientation of the chart, the multi-leveled interpretations available, and the application of this knowledge in living.

The natal chart, through the science of triangles, becomes a blue print, a schematic to be interpreted. The configurations of energy and forces describe our foundation, point to our walls, our heights of aspiration, and our dark cellar depths. Like a temple, a house, or a cathedral, the map of the potential for each life is drawn up and displayed for us. But having not taken Soul Architecture 101 we cannot read the blueprint. We cannot see that a particular habit is a wall that we keep bumping into, or that our deep caring that so often leads to depression is actually the stairway to our liberation. Through the triangulation of energies into which soul incarnated certain progress should result, certain applications of consciousness should happen. Certain truths or snippets of reality should shine through. Yet like light through a stained glass window these truths are colored and the light, though beautiful, is not pure.

Formation is an important seventh ray word. It speaks of a particular and precise order and the arrangement of things. With the small eye, precision might not be seen or the particularity of the order be recognized. But that does not negate its existence. The order and configuration of triangles, on any level including the human meditative ones, allows for a freer flow of specific energies or forces to specific areas for specific ends.

The formation of the Hierarchy and its externalization is certainly ordered and sequential. From the One - God, to The Manu, The Christ, and The Mahachohan, to the Seven Primary Masters,[49] and then to the widening circles of ashrams eventually numbering forty-nine, orderly and sequentially the Divine Intent of the Planetary Lord is being manifested. Parallel to this break down is that of the kingdoms and over arching it is the work of the Ray Lords, of which the Seven Masters are centers (chakras). Add to this the work of the Buddha, who in wisdom and compassion stays within this round of the Earth's evolution to anchor the will of God in a way not done before on this planet.

From the purest strata, down through the next, to the next, continuing to the densest (be that human or mineral) the potential idea of Deity works out. As it creates its scheme or grouping of activity the next dense level can be objectified. Group after group is created. This in itself is progress. But then progress begins from the bottom upward. Groups or individuals within the groups excel or attain and progress out of the paradigm in which they have lived and moved. Their being is beyond its confines. They move into the next level up or create a new grouping which is the next level up.

Consider Hierarchy. There is never a vacant place or position because there is always someone ready to step into the vacated place of attainment

---

[49] Occultly, there are more levels. These are being highlighted for simplicity sake.

by the on-going processes of attainment. Initiation at all levels negates "void" because initiation is undertaken only in consciousness of the lesser as well as the greater, and the need as well as the demand. One, like the Buddha, will stay in His or Her position until there is another ready and able (and always willing) to take that place.

As the numbers of semi-conscious and conscious workers expands the externalization process continues. The New Group of World Servers is comprised of both the semi-conscious and the conscious. Combining their strengths, in numbers and in heart, this group is changing the ways of humanity on a scale never seen before. Working with the fabric of everyday life, the New Group of World Servers slowly brings the new ideas of spirit into the daily living of humanity. Primarily through service of all kinds these workers are the good people who work for change. And there lies the definition of the NGWS. There are many good people in the human family, but the NGWS is an instrument of change and progress for the whole. Their united works affect whole groups of people and the consciousness of humanity. Examples might be, the Twelve Step Programs, Girl and Boy Scouts International, and The Red Cross. All bring to the recipients a measure of self-hood and responsibility for the self. These organizations also bring an education of the person and his relationship to the whole, as well as an example of selflessness.

The Seven Ray of Order, Organization, and Magic and Disciples

Order	creates	Systems of management of people, time, and resources
Seeing the Divine Pattern in one's life	brings	Sense of timing, cycles, flow with the seasons and currents available
Ritual	is	Creating sacred space; acknowledging the sacred
Formation and Reformation	creates	Revolutions and the transformation of whole systems, large and small
Practicality, Groundedness	leads to	Efficiency
Measuredness, conservative	leads to	Working within preset limits or formats

Figure 27

Chakras and Triangulation

Triangulation of the chakras is used extensively in healing and in the alignment of the personality to soul. Each chakra has a three-fold expression or use. Most of what is available about the chakras deals only with the matter or intelligence aspect. The soul, love, wisdom aspect and the will, spirit, design aspect is not much known. This vast subject would require a book in itself. Nonetheless we can broach it looking at one example thus expanding slightly the understandings of the chakric system and giving us another example of triangles.

The solar plexus is a chakra that is often spoken of negatively and referred to solely as a point of astrality. Most definitely the solar plexus is the point of our lower, mass psychism. It is a seat of our emotions and our astral nature. These few things are born of the knowledge aspect expressing through the chakra. Literally we gain knowledge of the world of feelings and sentiment through this center. We also grow the workings of the lower concrete mind, because the solar plexus is the place where kama and manas (desire and mind) come together and act as one. For most of our evolution we are a being of desire-mind. There is little or no separation between the two. This center is also the point that actively works at separating these two functions within the self. It is a long, hard, and painful ordeal. Once the separation is done and kama-desire and manas-mind are functioning independently, they can be re-integrated into the whole that will become the soul-infused personality.

For the disciple the solar plexus has a different function. Much less about worry, anxiety, or self-concern, the center of our lower sensitivities now becomes a way through which we perceive the worlds. The many kingdoms are open to the person who has moved through sentiment and can stand detached yet loving, compassionate and allowing. All life shares sentiency. This chakra is a processor of that sharing. This is the love wisdom level of the solar plexus.

For initiates this center represents the lowest point of spiritualized individuality in matter. The solar plexus becomes the anchor point, so to speak, of the personality, the heart the same for soul, and the crown for the spirit self (monad). The solar plexus has always been the primary point of recognizing our individuality, uniqueness, and differences from other people. Because of our sensitivity to one another on the most mundane levels we knew that one person made us happy, feel sad, hurt, deprived, or befriended. This same center then became the place of our caring, sharing, and awareness of the needs of others. Now, for the initiate, this center is the point of relationship and life en rapport. "All my relations"[50] is a Native American phrase that speaks of our relatedness to all of life. The solar plexus is the center of all our relations. Having separated out desire and mind, having accomplished their own relationship with soul thus experiencing "the marriage in the heavens," all that the initiate is and has is an offering and sharing of life giving quality and energy. The solar plexus becomes the point in the everyday worlds of men where those contributions can go out from and be received through. Again like begets like. And if most people are solar plexus oriented and polarized then the release from that polarization comes from two places. One is the heart - the next highest center, the other comes from the refined functioning of the solar plexus in another person. Unattached, unfettered, uncluttered, and unbothered, the initiate's poise beckons decorum. Elevation of consciousness and of the functioning of the chakra takes place.

The Seven Ray of Order, Organization, and Magic and the Initiates

Order	is	To be a conscious participant in the Divine Order, the Structure of the Plan and its expression
Magic	is	To be an agent of alchemical change in any environment or circumstance.
Transformation	is	To work within the constraints of form yet release the life/ consciousness contained therein.
Rhythm	is	At-one with the cycles of energy, time, and divine circulatory flow; the Tao.

---

[50] Mitakuye Oyasin means "we are all related" or "all my relations" in Lakota Sioux.

Intonation	is	The rhythmic repetition of the Word thus creating forms for the purposes of soul or spirit
Orientation	provides	consciousness that steers.
The Builder	makes	the Sacred apparent. Working with the Temple of Matter.

Group Progress is the Law of Elevation. In the elevation of consciousness three points are always working: the personalized consciousness, the point to be reached and penetrated, and the mind. The apex is obviously the penetrating or stretching point. It is that to which we aspire, that which we seek. The personalized consciousness is on any level, aspirant, disciple, or initiate. Even initiates of the highest degree are penetrating into levels of reality higher than those already assimilated. And the mind is the ground, the soil that will receive the seeds of insight, the water of truth, and the light of the soul or spirit sun.

Mountains are triangular in shape. The path of spiritual evolution has been likened to a mountain and initiation to being the result of living the arduous climb to the top. The symbols of this law are the mountain and the goat. The mountain of realization is only climbed by the shared pathways of Brotherhood. Together the seen and the unseen tread the way of the hearty with tireless effort. The agility of the goat is that of a gymnast, completely attuned to the contours of the slope, its jagged edges, its lofty heights. The goat is well suited to the climb, needing little food, and less drink. Its cashmere coat, coarse on the outside, keeps out the chill winds while the soft inner layer, prized by the world, traps the warmth of the heart. Yet most important for the goat's survival is her feet. Shaped like a triangle, three-sided and pointed, yet flat, she can stand on the smallest of spaces. Agile and nimble, she scales the cragged walls, undaunted, seemingly unaware of her precarious position. She seems unafraid.

And in some ways she is. The goat, like the disciple, treads only the ways known to her and known to her brethren. The herd has lived among these rugged rocks for generations. Its ways are recognized, like these laws of the soul and brotherhood.

Among us, living with us, are the Understanding Ones. Their light lifts our hearts, heals our wounds, and helps us with our burdens. Their teachings are often subtle and quiet, gentle and yet ever so powerful. We hear them with our hearts. Together we walk. Together humanity progresses, evolves, and is elevated to new heights of awareness. As one with each other, in unison, we climb the mountain, ascending into new light, a hierarchical light, the light of Immanence.

The systemic law at work within the Law of Group Progress is the Law of Vibration. All triangles, all ashrams, all work is made possible by the Law of Vibration and that from which it stems, the cosmic Law of Economy. An aspirant's or disciple's ability to work and the work one is able to do is completely in line with one's vibration and the degree to which one's rainbow bridge of consciousness, the antakharana, is tread or utilized. The vibrations within the ashram maintain its integrity, allow the readied chela to enter, and the readied Master to exit into greater fields of service. Finally, vibration is the very mathematical formula by which triangles are constructed and used. In all of these we see the Law of Economy working.

With the Law of Group Progress we have entered into true group awareness and true functioning of that which is group. The singular personality fades into the greater workings of the organic life of group and soul enterprises. And as we shall see with the remaining two laws even the individuality of the human soul begins to fade into the purposes of the One life.

Chapter Seven
The Sixth Law of the Soul
The Law of Expansive Response
"The Law of Breathing"[51]

A newborn babe sleeps. Silently, its chest rises and falls. Pure and beautiful this little body is kept alive because this child breathes. Yes, babies need food and a warm secure environment, but breathing it does for itself. The child needs no other to assist in that. Watch a baby breathe. And see the magic of the process. That simple statement of in-breath/Life, out-breath/existence is a meditation.

The Law of Expansive Response is the Law of Breathing that which is all around, that which is higher and more refined, that which is course and hard to take in, and that which is not yet a part of us but must be made so. The Law of Expansive Response requires that all that is available be brought into our self-expression and from there be breathed back out, now augmented by the qualities of life that are alive only within the individual that just breathed in. That process will expand every part and that, which is more expanded, will go out. Like a balloon, its function is not complete until it has been breathed into. Then it brings color and happiness to many. Like a wind instrument that is hollow and mute, the breath gives it the life of music. Like blowing the seeds of a dandelion puff or a milkweed pod, it is the breath that will distribute them to greater and fuller expression and thus give color and nectar to life.

The Law of Expansive Response pertains to the ever inclusive and growing areas of responsibility of the soul, whether those are human kingdom as a whole or the individual incarnating pilgrim. This responsibility

---

[51] The Tibetan Master DK gave a secondary name for each of the first five laws. I offer this secondary name for the Law of Expansive Response.

streams out of the symmetrical breathing process that is life lived as part of a greater life.

Symmetry means that which is above will become that which is below; that which is unseen will be made apparent; that which is vibrational will be given note and tone, cadence and expression. Symmetry, occultly, is the science of macro and micro, analogy, and co-measurement. Symmetry is not just the duplication of a design appearing on one side of a page and copied onto the other side. It is the intricacy of a butterfly wing that only becomes a display of beauty once the butterfly has breathed into the wet newly born wings and let them dry into solid form. Breath is equal in and out. Symmetry is the response to that equalizing breathing.

This law involves the ability of the initiate to reach and remain in the expansive planes of the spiritual triad, assimilate the totalities available, and then in wonderfully powerful and appropriate ways, incorporate these aspects of the real into everyday life. Expansive Response decrees that the ways of the Most High must become the skeletal structure behind the ways of the most common.

The spiritual triad can be considered the personality of the monad. But more accurately, the triad is the apparatus of the omniscience, omnipresence, and omnipotence of the spirit Self.

Omniscience	Omnipresence	Omnipotence
All-knowing	All-pervasive	All powerful
Manas	Buddhi	Atma

As a person grows in consciousness, these departments of reality open. Each is a totality in itself. Omniscience confers a vastness of knowledge and understandings, connections and correlations within matter and consciousness. Omnipresence instills, at first, the experience of God-ness everywhere and in all things, then blossoms into the revealed matrix of quality, energy, and rhythmic sequencing that makes all life appear, have reason, and disappear out of form. Omnipresence is a method of divine preservation. It includes conservation, expansion, infiltration, and annihilation. Omnipotence is the primal and inherent dynamic power that causes all to be, thus requires omnipresence and omniscience to know existence. Omnipotence self contains the laws of Majesty's expression. These laws, such a part of atmic consciousness, ensure that power used by deity and the spirit self can and will only be constructive in the larger sense. Destruction has a basic role and cycle, and is part of the building and sustaining processes of Life.

The person who can establish consciousness in these triadal realms, and reside there for periods of time, becomes imbued by omniscience, omnipresence, and omnipotence. The qualities of the triad shape-shift the mind into pure consciousness, re-make consciousness into a mixture of soul and spirit, and translate Life into a living expression of knowledge, clear reason and the geometric design of qualified light.

Expansive Response is the result of holding that state of consciousness. The individual is a portal through which the higher triadally understood and received realities descend. These known values or portions of the real must be conveyed, portrayed, displayed in ways that allow those who cannot reach or even know of spirit/Life's Plan to live and grow according to the unseen divine plan. One might ask of free-will. Is humanity's free will negated through the notion that there is a larger unseen intention toward which, like a leaf on a river, humanity flows?

Humanity moves in self-will not free-will. Its will is to empower the single self and its interests. Free-will is to move freely, unrestrained because one has mastered the realms of matter that are the ensphering walls of karma and circumstance. Free-will is to make a decision based on the real and the facts of the real; to be a part of a great body that chooses to flow with the least resistance because that serves the Life that is free. Free-will, then, is to participate fully in all of life; not to seek the way of separation and single self. Free-will is to live according to the laws of the Spirit, free from the fetters of matter's reverie and amnesia. It is to be free in conscious consciousness.

The Law of Expansive Response determines that for candidates for initiation[52], for initiates, and for those well within the magnetic aura of an ashram, there is no rest, only tension. This tension is the result of not only soul infusion but more so the infusion of electric fire streaming in from the spiritual heights. Electric fire is the highest fire; and it is best to put em-

---

[52] Conscious of that fact or not.

phasis on the word electric versus the word fire. It is too easy to let our mental data banks take this phrase and try to understand it via the mundane. That would be like gathering krill or plankton and thinking that we understand the blue whale.

Fire by friction, an aspect of matter, is the activity principle itself. Motion creates heat, heat or warmth is registered and creates more movement. Movement is a consumption of matter and the alchemy of it from one form and structure into a more basic form and structure. We are still left with a form – ash, smelted ore, digested food producing calories and body heat. Fire by friction can be measured in a multitude of ways (a hand on the forehead of someone with a fever, a thermometer in F, C, or K degrees, gamma radiation, magnitude of stars, the volume of water down a waterfall, or how often we need to replace our sneakers).

Solar fire, an aspect of consciousness, is the principle of light that runs through all levels of matter, including that which colloquially is called spirit. It is that which brings illumination, perspective, understanding, relation, and reason. Solar fire is warm to the consciousness, brings growth of awareness and selfhood. It is still yet pervasive and expansive.

Electric fire, an aspect of spirit, is the principle of Life, the spark of creation and design that makes all be. Electric fire is total in itself, self-containing the blue print of actualization, the choreography of externalization, the duration of manifestation, and the way of abstraction. Law, unyielding yet all creating, streams forth with electric fire. I-ness, not with singularity or ego, but I-ness that is Identity within all of creation is this fire. It is not about flame or color, consuming or reducing. It is not about heat or illumination. It is about the dynamic force that impels all to birth, expression, and completion within ItSelf – Spirit – the All.

The Third Ray of Active Intelligence and Adaptability

Creative Process	leads to	Flexibility with all types of Matter
The Mind of God	provides	Abstract Thought(s)
The Principle of Activity	creates	Rotary Motion
Economy in the use of Energy or matter	is	Divine Articulation
Giving form to ideas	births	Philosophy, Abstract Sciences, and Mathematics

Figure 28

Expansive response is just that - responding correctly to each expansive understanding, to each intuited whole, and being fully responsible for all that that entails. This is the working out of all of soul's intentions, not just a small part. It is the cascading effect of the waters of life from the monad pouring into the triad and seeking full expression in the worlds of men through the ways of soul. Soul can only work in expansive ways, ways that cause growth and awareness. These effects usually take time but soul is not deterred and monad stands impressing and unaffected.

Expansive response is pervasive. It is simple and gently powerful. It is so automatic that even the candidate for initiation often does not recognize how much of her life is governed by this law until she is in the thick of it. Every part of one's being is called to bear, work, expand, and respond appropriately. Thought becomes an act of magic setting certain things into action. Actions become teachings, the dharma given every moment to the world. Smiles and counsel are the blessings of the heart and offer the magic of soul simply.

One might say that disciples do this also and that aspirants attempt this with limited success. Why suggest that this law is for the initiated and those knowing the approachable vibration of the door?

There is an unmistakable aura of magnetism and compassion around those whose consciousness has expanded beyond meaning into purpose. There is a powerful presence born in unity, understanding, and patience that is not ruffled in the usual way of anger, jealousy, greed or separative thought. There is a knowing that glows in their eyes. It is the knowing of that which is beyond soul, of being able to tread the Way of Fire, of walking in the recognition of the All in each piece, each life, each heart, each breeze. This is beyond the disciple who increasingly lives in the light of soul and so seeks to serve the soul in all. This is a dream to the aspirant who still battles so with himself, his karma, and his desire to become.

The breath of soul is felt around initiates. There is a mysterious and delightful ease about them. Even in situations of difficulty they expand and respond, and so we respond to their impression.

They are like the invisible springs in a spring fed pond, constantly feeding the pond with freshness and life. They bubble newness and light into the whole of which they are a part. From the shore we cannot see these springs, but we do occasionally see the ripples on the surface as the fresh bubbles rise. We can taste the sweetness of the rich water, revel in its clarity and translucence as we watch sunbeams dance on its surface.

The light that they give is simple, easy to comprehend, born in the heart, spoken in essential phrases, unfettered by social morays and cultural distinctions. Yet the profundity and all pervasive quality of their words, their deeds begets response. It expands within each person's ear, heart and mind. Eventually, sometimes instantaneously, change results. Growth in soul and therefore in spirit happens.

Examples of their work remain with us. These offerings were the responses of individuals or groups to divine ideas available and ready to be precipitated into the three worlds of men. The ideas, concepts, beauty, and portions of truth that these forerunners put into form expanded human ways of thought, consciousness, business and economy, science and psychology, government and law. With that list we merely name the obvious arenas of their influence; influence that is still expanding today. Thoughts are alive and are beings themselves, as Master Morya in the *Agni Yoga* series of books often tells us. Aligned and perceptive, these people penetrated the realms of waiting thoughts and ideas. The thoughts expanded their consciousness. More importantly, through them and their work these thought-entities have been allowed to expand the consciousness of the entire human kingdom. The attentive ones were able to tap the fountains of life that each idea waiting in the Mind of God could offer a particular time in history, group of people, or echelon of life.[53]

Listing just a few of them by category might be the simplest way to recognize how much of the way we live our lives is colored by the expanding breaths of this law of the soul.

Religion and the ways of the soul and spirit: Akhenaten, Melchizedek, Moses, Gautama Buddha, Jesus Christ, Mohammed, St. Francis, Martin Luther, Brigham Young, Sri Aurobindo, Mother Theresa.

Philosophy and our search for the meaning of life: Solomon, Confucius, Lao Tze, Plato, Aristotle, Socrates, Plotinus, Descarte, Goethe, Rudlolf Steiner, Rousseau, Voltaire, Locke, Thoreau, Bertrand Russell, Marx, Chief Seattle, Martin Luther King, Kuebler-Ross, Freud, Jung.

Politics and government: Constantine, Jefferson, Peter the Great, Lincoln, Roosevelt, Gandhi, Mao Tse-tung.

Sciences: Euclid, Pythagoras, Ptolemy, Copernicus, Galileo, Paracelsus, Da Vinci, Bacon, Harvey, Linneus, Curie, Newton, George Washington Carver, Jung, Einstein, Heisenberg, Hawkings.

Arts: the myth creators in all lands, the ancient artisans whose names we will never know but whose work in form, color, technique, and spirit is the foundation upon which all art forms stand. Homer, Shakespeare, Poe, Giotto, Michelangelo, Cezanne, Corot, Masaccio. In literature and in the creation of art forms many more names could be sighted. Musically also the list of forerunners and those who opened the heavens of music could be long. Bach, Mozart, Beethoven, Stravinsky are but some of the obvious few.

Others who could fit in many categories: Columbus, Edison, Bell, Ford, Harriet Tubman, Fredrick Douglas, Margaret Sanger, Marco Polo, Benjamin Franklin.

(It is interesting to note that the categories of science and the arts could easily be lengthy. We are reminded that humanity is an expression of the fourth and fifth rays, the rays of art [harmony through conflict] and science.)

---

[53] A friend offered the thought of "ideas hovering as living entities and moving outward to impregnate whole civilizations, centuries, or decades…"

Each of these individuals breathed deep of the Mind or Heart of God. Each of them was touched by the Life which is in all of life. That can never be contained in the life of one person, let alone one person's heart or mind. They, and many others that we can all think of, breathed it out to the world. We are still breathing the changes brought into the quality of our living. Each of these gifts has become the threads of the fabric of humanity. Most of these people are known to us all. Little need be said about the life giving breath that they fostered. The names of some, however, might not be recognized but the fruit of their works will be.

Akhenaten, a young Egyptian pharaoh, attempted to bring monotheism, the realization of one loving creator god, and the beginnings of democracy to Egypt in the mid 1300's BC. He is considered by some Egyptologists to be the first pacifist, realist, humanitarian, and the first person to attempt to found a religion based upon a God of love.

Brigham Young saved the infant Mormon Church through leadership, organization, and determination. Though predominately an American Christian sect, their missionary work has spread throughout the world. Strong beliefs in family, morality, that God is a developing being and that man progresses toward a state of being god-like himself are cornerstones to the Mormon religion.

Mother Theresa was a strong female in a mainly patriarchal religion. It is interesting that her work of selfless, tireless service for the poor and sick spoke louder than the pomp and circumstance of the Catholic Church. Like St. Francis and St. Claire in their day, she offered an example of humility and grace.

Lao Tze gave us the Tao te Ching (pronounced dow day ching), an understanding of the Universe, of God, and of the human struggle, and the simplicity of "non-being" that is the completeness of Being. From him we have non-action that Gandhi and the people of India used against the British as they sought freedom. Non-violent protests and practioners of civil disobedience also stem from the Tao.

Plotinus is generally considered the founder of Neoplatonism, containing within it the thought of this trinity: "the One" - an indefinable ultimate principle, the soul, and the dark unreality of matter. According to Plotinus the goal of the human soul is to return to the One. His teachings had a strong influence on both Christian and Islamic thought.

Descarte is called the founder of modern philosophy. Locke gave us Empiricism of Thought and Liberalism in politics. Undoubtedly Marx's original ideas of socialism and community-ism will find fresh soil in the Aquarian age. Chief Seattle reminded us that we do not own the earth, only that we share it with all other creatures. Furthermore, he asked how one people can take from other people that which does not belong to either, but by divine gift is here for all. By our interrelatedness all and everything suffers as the balance is tipped in any direction.

Da Vinci's art will always remain exemplary, but his contributions to anatomy, botany, and mechanics permeated the scientific world of his day and became the substructure for many who would come after him. Bacon opened the philosophy of science. Harvey theorized and confirmed the way in which blood circulates in the human body, thus becoming the founder of modern physiology. George Washington Carver was a black American botanist and chemist who helped bring prosperity to large areas of the impoverished southern United States.

In the arts Kandinsky is considered the originator of abstract art, Corot of impressionism, and Cezanne of cubism. Poe deserves more credit than any other writer for the transformation of the short story from anecdote to art. He virtually created the detective story and perfected the psychological thriller. Most of the books read and most of the movies seen by the public today fall into these two categories.

Then there are the people who belong to many categories and might be called liberators. Henry Ford gave us the assembly line and brought us out of the horse and buggy era. Harriet Tubman, an abolitionist, engineered the Underground Railroad that smuggled American slaves to freedom. Margaret Sanger coined the phrase "birth control," created the Planned Parenthood Federation, and educated women and society to the fact that women were dying at the rate of tens of thousands per year from birth, self-induced abortions, and exhaustion from having too many children. And Benjamin Franklin was a fountain of practical everyday inventions that we are wearing (spectacles - glasses), receiving (the postal service copied all over the world), and being warmed by (the franklin stove - a self-contained, free-standing wood stove). He is considered to have discovered electricity, and as a diplomat obtained necessary funds from the French to sustain the American Revolutionary war. The United States might not be here and I might not be typing on this computer were it not for Franklin's work.

The living breath that each offered circulates still. It was born of the ability to penetrate, perceive, and hold the necessary point of tension and see it through. This breath was born of the "power which maketh all things new. It lives and moves in those who know the self as one."[54] As a result of the Way of Fire, the way of electric will, the way of the soul aspiring to monadic heights, power and love, peace and presence blend. Response is appropriate and engenders the new. All awareness is ever expansive and breaks into new paradigms of reality and totality. The limits are only the mind space. But the Buddhist phrase of "a sky-like mind" can give perspective as to just how expansive an individual's mind can be and the vastness it, with training in expansive responsiveness, can apprehend.

Though not all the examples listed are initiates, most are or were. Some of these people had not broken free of the dis-eases of life in matter. But most had found the Way of freedom and breathed it into the collective of humanity.

The Third Ray of Active Intelligence and Adaptability and the Masses

Activity	leads to	Scatteredness; busy-ness
Intelligence	creates	Thought about action, but not taking action
Manipulation	leads to	Bending the truth to suit one's needs or desires
Adaptability	leads to	The ability to make any environment livable
Being selective	leads to	Learning to make choices based on personal return

Figure 29

---

[54] This is a line from a mantram given by the Tibetan for world service. It has been adapted a few times for different purposes. See appendix for the whole mantram.

The Third Ray of Active Intelligence and Adaptability and Disciples

Inquiry	leads to	Questioning and arriving at a higher truth or an underlying cause
Activity	leads to	Multi-tasking, in either the objective or subjective worlds
Creative Ability	leads to	Using what is at hand to best suit the need
Abstract Mind	provides	The ability to bring concepts into a useful form

Figure 29

The initiates live a triple freedom. Not freedom from the three worlds, the three basic vehicles (physical, emotional, mental), or the three corresponding planes. Their freedom is not a freedom *from* anything. It is the freedom of; of being able to reside, participate, and then express the intuited knowledge or revealed ideas of the higher triad, of Manas - the Mind of God, of Buddhi - the Heart and Reason of God, and of Atma - the Intention of God. Freedom from is no longer important. Perfection, as the aspirant would consider it, is no longer relative. Service, the desire and method of the disciple, is no longer a thought. It is ingrained in the breath of the initiates. With increasing facility they roam the pathways of the intangible - feeling, hearing, seeing and knowing the Mighty presence veiled by the everyday, by the clouds and mists of time and space, by the relativity of a life. Their union now is not the pairs of opposites of the personality and soul but a union of soul and monad.

Tension, tension, and tension again. That is the way for all initiates. At each point of contact, during each moment of tension, they create the ripples that go outward to the world, yet they remain intact, serene, and poised. Toward this all work, not for self though obviously one benefits, but for the whole, the work, the Plan.

Response-ability is the end product. Right response to any given situation, the right use of any and all forces available, the right understanding of the circumstance, its beginnings and causes, its working out and fruition. Able to walk in the triadal light, the past, present, and future all become relative. Karma is revealed and understood. Compassion and patience fill the mind and heart of the initiates because they know. Knowing, serenity is in them and all around them.

In all of this is a stillness. Their serenity grows out of this stillness. It is because of stillness that expansiveness is produced. It is in stillness that the attentive and penetrating disciple realizes the truth that thought and motion are ultimately one. Breathing, they become aware of the combination of stillness and expansion, of activity and confinement. Further, there is the realization that breath was not only the path of these two dichotomies, but what unifies them as well.

Where there is stillness and activity, the Knower and the Known, there is the Third Ray. Where there is tension there is attention and the right acknowledgment of all that is at hand, all that can be recognized and utilized. This is Divine Manipulation. Out of this all magic issues. From this all responsibility stems. With this, all souls work as the manipulatives of the monad, the outpost of the triadally conscious Self.

The Third Ray of Active Intelligence and Adaptability and Initiates

Adaptability	is	To build that which reveals Divine Purpose
Comprehension	is	To relate Space and Time
Memory	reveals	That all things have a cause
To Produce Thought	is	To produce Form
Stillness	is	The Spider at the Center waiting to be engaged
Synthesis	is	The Center of the Web of Thought

Figure 30

The Third Ray is the ray of the many. From the examples of workers given earlier, it is easily seen that effects were multiple and far reaching. The Third Ray is also considered a ray of time. These contributions from human beings en rapport with the Mind of God have lasted and become part of the fabric of our world. We live today with the results and growth of work put in motion, in some cases, thousands of years ago.

The Third Ray is the ray of adaptability. In each case, matter was adapted to fit the needs of the spirit impression. In each case an idea was brought into creative expression and demonstration. In each case, and thousands more that were not offered as examples, the disciple/initiate was the arbiter of divine economy and we, all of humanity, were profoundly affected thereby. The breathing process can be seen so clearly. Their work still breathes in our lives.

Breathing. How innate and little understood this magic is. Each breath is in fact the inspiration of countless cells, dimensions of reality, and the manifestation of a divine intention; as simple as the intention to stay in the form and as exalted as the intention to create.

The in-breath is an invocation. It is also a gathering of all that is required to accomplish a goal: all mental substance, ideas, creative thought processes, and awareness of corresponding results; the gathering of astral matter, all feelings about the intended design, all color, sound, and felt sense of it, and the love necessary to give it life because Love is the greatest power; and vitality gathered from the etheric plane. This vitality (prana/chi) will ensure that once this creation is breathed forth it will live in whatever realm or matter is its destination and function.

Consider Harriet Tubman and the Underground Railroad. At each step of the way she had to keep the intention of the work: freedom to slaves, without injury and or unnecessary danger to helpers and way station owners along route. People had to house, feed, provide clothing and money to each slave smuggled along the Underground Railroad. Harriet Tubman had to maintain not only the vision and idea of this freedom train, but keep all the people involved quiet, courageous, and trusting. The resources of people, land, barns, animal transport, trail keepers and scouts, along with sympathetic whites wealthy and poor all had to be coordinated and constantly shifted around so that no one trail or group of people were used too often or repeatedly in a short period of time. She breathed her will into this endeavor. Her strength, stamina, cunning intelligence, and stout heart are what magnetized all those who worked together in this effort. Her alignment with soul is unquestioned.

As we look to the sun shining in the sky we see this law in action. Each molecule within the sun's Heavenly body is alive with electric fire. And each atom is at such a point of conscious tension that its influence is both extensive and expansive. It breathes and radiates, magnetizing all within this solar system. Because of that life-giving essence, every atom within this solar system responds, to both the tension and the expansion. Every particle of consciousness grows in kind with the growth and expansion of the sun's consciousness. This process becomes a beautiful dance of reciprocal motion and returned elevations of meaning - feeding the fire within each part, burning limitations, freeing each other, back and forth, over and over. The sun breathes a qualified breath. Everything that inhales that life sustaining breath grows, expands, and lives more consciously. Then they breathe, and their exhalations return to the sun. These are breaths of conscious expansion in matter. The sun receives and expands because the cell within His body (the person, the group, the kingdom, Hierarchy, etc) has received and expanded with the breath that the Sun God had sent forth. Over and over again, the whole and the part dance a cosmic minuet, elegant and symmetrical.

It is electric fire to which the Old Commentary refers in the beautiful stanza given to us by the Tibetan regarding this law.

> "The Sun, in all its glory, has arisen and cast its beams athwart the Eastern sky. The union of the pairs of opposites produce, in the cycles of the time and space, both clouds and mists. These veil a mighty conflagration....
>
> The flood pours forth. The ark floats free...the flames devour. The three stand free; and then again the mists envelop.

> Above the clouds of earth, a sign shines forth... Only the eye of vision sees this sign. Only the heart at peace can hear the thunder of the Voice which issues from the dark depths of the cloud. Only an understanding of the law which elevates and lifts can teach the 'man of fire and son of water' to enter into mist. From thence he climbs on to the mountain top and there again stands free."[55]

The pair of opposites, the waters of life and the fluidity of matter, (spirit/matter) create clouds of forgetfulness and mists of temporal forms. These veil the "mighty conflagration" of the inner essence, the spark of the Divine that is the soul, itself veiling the monad's flaming beauty.

"The flood pours forth. The ark floats free...the flames devour." The flood of soul waters has uplifted the personality self. It, the ark, the temple, the vessel, floats free from the pulls of worldliness. It floats above the waters on which it was tossed for centuries. It floats above the desert, barren of conscious living, incarnation after incarnation. It floats free from the misuses of itself in misunderstanding the laws of life, soul, and the cosmos. Freely the soul infused personality moves in the electric air of light. The flames of purification, refinement and integration have devoured before.

Now the flame that burns is electric, a flame of Will and Power. It is the flame of initiation burning within the consciousness of the candidate devouring him or her until she is the door, transfigured, renounced or master.[56] This electric fire consumes the identity of all parts of the self, though they already are identified with the Source of their being, until "only the One Who Is remains."[57] "The three stand free," the three of soul-infused personality, triadal consciousness, and monadic totality, free to be a coherent functioning whole, ready once again to "tread the ways of men and

---

[55] *Esoteric Psychology, Vol. II*, pg. 199, by Alice A. Bailey. Lucis Publishing Co. New York.
[56] Three levels of initiate: transfigured – third degree, renounced – fourth, and master – fifth.
[57] *Esoteric Psychology, Vol. II*, pg. 341.

know the ways of God[58]." And so "again the mists envelop" and the initiate incarnates, or continues with the work already in progress during an incarnation. The mists are the temporal in which we all must work. They are the mass of illusions perpetrated by humanity as a whole, the dream state (or nightmare) in which most of our brothers and sisters live. The sun augments the fire; it dissipates the mist and dries the earth. And thus the work is done.

From here we can ponder the systemic Law of Fixation. The initiate's orientation is "fixed" in the monad. This is the ultimate resolution of the pairs of opposites – the initiate is the matter aspect resolved and at-one with the spirit. This is the assimilation of synthesis, and the concretization of the Absolute in the world. The Law of Fixation deals with pin point accuracy, and here in conjunction with the Law of Expansive Response, it deals with entireties, with right manipulation, right response, total responsibility that is the ability to respond totally in ever increasing areas. The old adage holds true that "with increased knowledge comes increased responsibility." It is the basis of the Law of Expansive Response.

The Law of Fixation is also key to the magic that a worker of light will try to accomplish; that which he has come to know, and therefore is part of, must be externalized, and given a form of some kind (thought, feeling, color, action, creation, demonstration). Fixation is to anchor it first in consciousness, and then bring it down through the planes of matter, keeping it true as an expression of the original idea or realization.

Cosmic law takes on an active part in the consciousness of the initiate. The Law of Synthesis, governing the Path of Initiation, is the alpha and omega of this law. Out of it the Absolute spins taking on the mists of veiled form as it descends into matter. And back to the synthesis of the absolute it returns, spinning in electric fire, burning off the veils, revealing its total light, giving all who can reach the triadal heights the opportunity to "with the eye of vision see the sign... (and) hear the thunder of the Voice which issues from the dark depths of the cloud...The sun augments

---

[58] From the Mantram of Unification. See appendix for whole text.

the fire; it dissipates the mist and dries the earth. And thus the work is done."[59]

---

[59] Esoteric Psychology, Vol. II, pg. 199, by Alice A. Bailey; Lucis Publishing Co. New York, NY.

Chapter Eight
The Seventh Law of the Soul
The Law of the Lower Four
"The Law of Free Standing"[60]

The Law of the Lower Four describes liberation from the prison of matter. It stems from the occult fact that there are seven levels to Life, and that Life has chosen to differentiate via the rule of sevens. More clearly stated, with the seven there will always be three above, three below and one in between. The one in the middle is the bridge between the refined and the coarse, between the redeemed and the unredeemed, between the spirit of life and the forms that life has taken.

Always the fourth is the one in the middle. It is the balancing point. Because of that it is the level of supreme struggle and conflict. It has its feet in the three levels below but sees, feels, or senses the reality in the three above, and for both there is love. There is also indecision. Yet, when the fourth level of expression has been passed through, we stand free from the pulls of matter and begin to become an adept in the ways of spirit or soul through matter. And this is true no matter what plane, what part of the path, or what the quality that has been part of soul's training.

Moving through the three lower divisions of matter we learn what matter is. This is done through the experiences of its confinement. With the fourth, we have endured four/sevenths of that matter's expression. We have lived through more than half of what is contained or being offered within that realm. We now move onto the higher and more refined levels of that quality or realm and into the more liberated aspects of those same qualities. That first half lies behind us. It no longer holds us. A river half

---
[60] The secondary name that I offer for this law.

crossed is almost forded. A quality 4/7ths incorporated into the self is well rooted and has become a known part of the equipment. A person who has worked through the integration of the physical, astral, and mental parts of the self and is now, through their coordination, standing as a personality in the worlds is someone who can use those three parts of himself more than being used by them, including the forces that comprise them.

The fourth level is the one of the most hardship and pain. The fourth ray is the ray of struggle and conflict, feeling the burden deeply and concretely. The fourth subplane within any plane is the realm of the most confusion, forces battling each other, both the higher and the lower seeking to lure the disciple. It is the place of half and half, half dark/half light, half intuited/half illusory. It is a realm where most things can be seen to have a function, a worth, and a reason. But many of the reasons stream out of our thoughts of the temporary and the current situation. Much of the worth stems from our desires, dreams, hopes, and wishes. Most of the function is a product of inertia and the status quo that is of matter itself. The truth and beauty that are the creators of the form lie in the three levels above this place of the swinging pendulum. They lie literally on the other side.

At some point the individual stops the pendulum from swinging and decides that the only course to take is out of the partial, the temporary, or the status quo and dare to move forward. Forward is upward. Upward is into the light of the higher three levels. This is an act of will with all of the person's equipment galvanized into making this movement. Will is what will see the step through, and the person will leave the lower behind by creating the bridge of resolve.

We can imagine beginning from the bottom and that with each level a block or wall is erected out of the matter of that level. As we move through the fourth we stand encased in a prison four-square of our own making (consciously or unconsciously so). It is this recognized imprisonment that is the source of much of the bewilderment, powerlessness, frustration, and the eventual deep felt need for change. We must break free from the prison, but the walls cannot be broken down. Instead, after much distress, the eye looks up and it is realized that the only way out is through ascension. That act of levitation will require resolve, stillness and coordination of all parts of the self, plus a supreme act of will. If accomplished, this person will stand free from matter and become a builder of light.

No initiation is taken until after this fourth level is resolved. This law decrees the border over which we, as souls, are considered free from the trappings of matter. Having crossed over the bridge connecting the three levels or planes of expression below to the three levels or planes above, the soul has made a monumental step. It has cast off the chains that bind one to matter's overriding influence and has stepped into the light of day, the day of spirit and soul-ness.

The Law of the Lower Four is just that - having passed through the lower four we arrive at the fifth. The fifth is the quintessence of anything and everything. Yet, this entry into the higher fifth does not mean perfection; it means only accomplishment. The totality of a plane, quality, or part of the self is not yet encompassed by the consciousness of the soulfull person. This fact is the reason for initiates not being perfect. There are still three subplanes of matter to learn to command, to live within, consciously and unbounded.

For example, a person who is preparing for the second initiation is working primarily with astral and concrete mental matter. In order to achieve the necessary level of astral quiescence and positive polarity she must understand and be free to move within the lower four subplanes of the astral plane. Going through that tremendously trying and testing ordeal requires some objectivity. This is born of the mind. It requires detachment, discipline, and coolness of response in contradistinction to reactiveness - qualities also born of the mind. Having arrived on the other side of this battlefield she is freed from the downward pull and allure of the lower astral plane. She will move more in the way of response and inspiration; and because there are still 3/7ths of the astral plane to completely understand and command, she will still occasionally stumble and fall into the mire of anger. She will sometimes react inappropriately. We remember again that *initiation is permeation not perfection.* It is a lengthy process with many seasons.

The same applies for the third and fourth degrees. And it has been offered by the Tibetan Master DK that one of the last negative mental tendencies to be purged is that of irritation. This is accomplished with the fifth degree of mastership. Furthermore, he offers the thought that illusion is a factor until at least the sixth initiation. These points of non-perfection for even the "perfected" are evidence of small portions of matter within certain planes or certain nuances within a quality that have not yet been perfectly understood, assimilated, and synthesized into the expanded consciousness.

Any plane of matter and its seven subplanes. Counting from below or above.

7	Subplane related to Atma	purest expression of matter	1
6	Subplane related to Buddhi	the light of the matter itself	2
5	Subplane related to the Soul	achievement	3
4	Battlefield, or burning ground	Kurukshetra in the Gita	4
3	Ring-pass-not of how this matter moves densely	knowledge of this matter	5
2	The attractiveness of matter	desire for matter's enticements	6
1	Matter's densest power	form-boundedness, crystallization	7

Figure 31

Five is related to the mental plane, the consciousness, and soul. It is on the fifth subplane (counting from the bottom) that the meanings of things, the reason for their appearances, and the mystery that lies back of all expression begins to dawn on the will-imbued individual. Interestingly it is not the fourth ray that this law primarily uses but the fifth, the Ray of Concrete Knowledge or Science. This, the last law of the soul, utilizes a ray that is part of soul's primary nature. The kingdom of souls is an expression of rays Two and Five. Through long sojourns soul has experimented with matter; often the incarnating jiva has been lost in the minutia that the fifth ray knows so well. Or it has denied the very existence of life intangible and sought only the security of that which could be seen, touched, and smelled. All this is of the three lower levels of existence on a plane of expression. But then the quest for mystery began, for the flame of life in all things, for that something that makes all life tick to a rhythm not conditioned by man. Long a prisoner of the matter that she gathered around herself, the person feels confined. The gaze too long has been down, into the apparent. Is not the atom invisible to the naked eye? Is not magnetism a creator of direction? The eye is lifted off the tangibility of matters mundane and begins to look for evidence of the unseen Real.

The Fifth Ray of Concrete Knowledge or Science

Understanding and the use of knowledge	brings	Practicality
Mental Illumination	brings	Clarity
Uncovering the Mysteries of Life	leads to	Discovery
Revelation and Light	leads to	The Reasons Why
Methodology	brings	Sequencing
Interested in and Attending to Details	lets	The Small Reveal the Great

Figure 32

A scene is given to us in the Fifth Ray stanza for the Direction of Repulse in *Esoteric Psychology*, Vol. II.[61] In the four-square bottom of a pyramid a person sits among his instruments of science. His gaze is ever upon that which lies before him. He seeks to understand the ways of matter and the ways of life, but after time unmeasured his frustration is so painful that he lifts his eyes up and cries out for help. His eyes are transfixed on the triangle shape of the top of the pyramid and eventually the apex point in the center. In this moment of positive meditative tension the point of the pyramid opens and light streams into the prison-like base where sits the frustrated incarnated soul. The mystery of light, of life, and of the soul as the midway point between matter and spirit dawns upon the imprisoned one. And as he breathes with this revelation a golden key descends through a shaft of light and falls onto the worker's table. The key

---

[61] *Esoteric Psychology, Vol. II*, pg. 169.

will unlock the prison doors of his limited mind and his sense boundedness. The key is the omniscience of the soul, all knowing of the seen and unseen, tangible and concrete as well as the tangibility of the subtle realms. The key is light itself, the illuminating factor, born of awareness gathered through the life experiment called experience.

It is also a key of Quintessence. At the fourth initiation the soul essence itself is liberated from the aeonal immersion in the lower three planes of matter (physical, astral, mental). Soul stands on the fourth plane of spirit's expression, buddhi, the plane "whereon form dies", equally then the plane whereon form is born.

Held within the golden temple (causal body) created over centuries the soul knows its limitedness. Though the walls are made of the finest substance, and have been built from the most rarefied experiences, it still is a limitation to the spirit-aware-Self. The soul is the midway point, like the fourth subplane, between spirit and matter. The soul, then, is the cross: vertically aligned, and horizontally serving. The soul is ever at the point of tension that is the center of the cross where the lines of both impression and expression meet. As the fourth degree approaches, a fullness of knowing the multitudinous manifestations and permutations of life in matter, and matter's response to life, is the mind of the initiate. A fullness of the love "which passeth understanding" and "maketh all things new" is equally and experientially known. Now, a full life lived in the will of the greater Intentions of Life by Life move this soul. The tension of being a manifesting soul at the center of the cross with its four extended points has grown and is almost complete. Its completion will mark a new set of four, no longer the four of matter confining, but matter redeemed.

The crucifixion, the fourth initiation, could quite possibly be the deepest struggle any human being will know; and this for good reason. This person is a true human being, living light, love, and the unity of brotherhood. They have lived, remember their living, served, and suffered as do all their brothers and sisters. But this person also knows the burden of the world, of God, and the inner cries for freedom given up by not only this kingdom but by the others. Simultaneously all that remains unrefined and unresolved must be dealt with. Most importantly, it must be dealt with alone. For the fourth degree the person will mount the cross created out of the very Self that he or she is. He will give all that is, all that he thinks is left, and will find that there is even more to give. This person will then take all that she can carry of the burden of the world, the unredeemed of humanity and will place it upon her heart. And lastly this initiate will open his mind to the darkened thought forms that humanity has created, engendered, and maintained for generations. Alone on her self-made cross this person will descend into humanity's darkness and dross, and the final interminable Dark Night of the Soul will ensue. All light will be blotted out by the unredeemed matter of all the planes that soul can touch. The inner sky will grow dark. The pain of soul will be endured.

The Fifth Ray of Concrete Knowledge or Science and the Masses

Inquiry	leads to	Skepticism
Methodical	leads to	Following procedure without flexibility
Linearity	leads to	Literality
Detail Orientation	leads to	Narrow focus
Concrete Knowledge	creates	Development of a data base, recognized knowledge
Clarity	leads to	The ability to reason
Discrimination	leads to	The ability to know fact from fiction

Figure 33

Myths through the ages have given us the story of the hero descending into the underworld and freeing the imprisoned ones held there. The Law of the Lower Four is the reason for those myths. The hero, the soul, must first free herself from the trappings of matter but then must always return to free the others still trapped. Hercules entered Hades to free Prometheus. Buddha battled Mara, the dark god of illusion. Christ, placed in a tomb, descended into the very body of the Earth and brought the light of freedom to all forms of life, not just the human.

From the Old Commentary we are given this ancient hint about the Law of the Lower Four.

"Four sons of God went forth. But only one returned. Four Saviors merged themselves in two, and then the two became the One."[62]

Four sons of God refers to the incarnating soul as it lives and realizes its experiments and existence in the four levels of matter (etheric/physical, astral, mental, personality identity). These are passed through before the living expression is soul-being. Only one returned, that is the soul-infused and transfigured personality. It now is free in in the ways of matter, the ways of men, and in the ways of God. Permeated by the Light, radiating the will of spirit through the light of soul, this person has learned of matter and stands free from entrenchment.

Four Saviors are the one of the transfigured initiate and the three of the Spiritual Triad - Manas, Buddhi, Atma. They, at and with the fourth initiation, merge themselves in the ultimate resolution of duality for a human being. Soul released, at-oned, the duality is now:

spirit-Father-monad   and   instrument-matter-son.

And with the fifth initiation the two will become the One, the master of compassion and champion of liberation.

The Fifth Ray of Concrete Knowledge or Science and Disciples

Clarity	brings	Illumination
Procedure	ensures	Enlightened Living of the Path
Detail Orientation	provides	Ability to work accurately in matter
Questioning	leads to	Discovery of the Real
Mystery	leads to	Self-forgetfulness, focus is not the individual
Discrimination	leads to	Right action, right effort

Figure 34

There are a number of fours that have helped humanity grow. In the 7th century BC, the Buddha put forward the Four Noble Truths. The crux of this teaching is that humanity suffers and creates karma because it desires. Both chain us to the wheel of rebirth. Incarnating time and time again, we desire, and continue the chain linking. Be free from desire and free oneself from the wheel, thus liberation and true compassion. These cannot be known until desire is superceded. In the 6th century Pythagoras put forth his intuited system of number[63]: Monad/Unity, Dyad/Duality, Triad/Harmony = Kosmos/ordered world. Christ's teachings are offered through the four gospels.[64] The teaching on the four worlds in the Kabbala, and the four points on each of the three crosses in astrology, each provide huge windows into quality, tendencies, and understanding.

There is another "four" that is very ancient, possibly given in the Mystery Schools of Hermes and brought down to us through Hermeticism. The Tibetan mentions it in the rules for white magic.[65]

"To Will. To Know. To Dare. To be Silent."

These four injunctions move the disciple/initiate forever into the point of tension that is manifestation or externalization. These four phrases can apply to each of the four personal vehicles (personality, mind, astrality, phys/etheric body). Also, with this law of the soul, they can apply to the soul, buddhi, atma, and monad.

The Soul – the Son of Mind wills to live the will of the greater soul and group or the monad, its father in heaven. Soul is the source of will for the persona, but at this level, the soul is the participant in a greater life and will. The soul wills to be the intercessor, the middle principle and thereby enter the heights in order to bring light, life, and consciousness to the

---

[62] Ibid, pg. 200.

[63] Most people know of the Pythagorean Theorem learned by all children in elementary school. But Plato, in the Doctrine of Divine Forms, proselytized Pythagoras' system. Pythagoras, along with Euclid is one of the two fathers of geometry.

[64] There are non-canonized gospels as well. It is possible that some of these are closer to the real sayings and teachings of Christ since they have not been changed. The four canonical gospels have been adulterated a number of times for political reasons over the last 2000 years.

[65] *A Treatise on White Magic* pg. 287 by Alice A. Bailey. Lucis Publishing Co. New York.

depths. The soul also wills to hold all that is necessary - energy, force, and multiple types of matter - thereby working white magic, the alchemical magic of the soul.

Buddhi is to know all, not in the way of the mind ever limited by the tendency of concretion, but to know through the ability of rapport, energetically and essence-tially understood. This knowing is to live light and to experience how light is sound, vibration, tone, and the divine Word that creates all incarnations of form. Buddhi is the design that becomes the Plan and makes itself known and revealed through the manifested ideas of the human kingdom as well as all presentations of beauty and form in the other kingdoms. Buddhi is not the mind. It is not limited by the tendencies of form. It is the malleability of sound itself. Light cannot be seen if a wall or curtain blocks it, but sound can be heard through wall or veil. Sound has the "Doppler effect", that is to say that we experience its changeability, its interaction with space/time. We hear sound be condensed, compressed, or expanded. The same effect is lost on sight unless we naturally have infra-red or ultra-violet vision.

Buddhi contains the fluidity of all form. Buddhi is the "plane whereon form dies". Equally it is the plane whereon form is born. All archetypes, all divine ideations will move through the sounding resonance of buddhi's vibrational alchemy and be born onto the plane of Manas. There it will take shape, color, and movement according to what is vibrationally contained, in other words, the contexts of knowledge contained in Manas.

Buddhi is the plane where most of Hierarchy finds its ranks, councils, and work. This place of highest Neptunian water, is the plane where the Will of God becomes. It becomes the Plan that all ashrams will execute to the best of their abilities. The interconnectedness of Hierarchy can only exist in the geometrical light orchestration that is Buddhi. "To Know" is just that. An initiate knows because he or she is a participant in the work, from its inception in the buddhic Clouds of Realization down to the dense manifestation on earth.

"To dare" refers to Atma. The initiate must first dare to enter the stream of electric fire that is Atma, then dare to reside in consciousness long enough to have that fire permeate and as a result fundamentally change his or her mind. Relation with and in the plane of Atma is totally wordless, conceptless, and is instead a Now of Identification, hence a communing. Communication was left, even in high telepathic and unadulterated forms, on the plane of buddhi. That total and essential truth and knowing grew the consciousness into a level of inclusivity hard to know outside of buddhi. But atma is not about relation, rapport,[66] or quality. Atma is Law. Law, atmically identified, has to do with creation itself, how Life creates out of its very substance, how there is only One Life, regardless of the illusion of duality. Law is freedom, and freedom is law; the freedom to enter the lower realms and be destroyed, as well as the freedom to destroy any encasing form[67] and be free.

Atma is a plane of fire, electric and self-consuming[68]. Like the biblical image of the burning bush, never decreased or consumed, atma is the totality of realized completion. It is the plane of fohat's first decent from the willed breath of Spirit/monad. *Fohat* is the arrow of destiny, the alpha and omega of all thingness, the initial spark that causes all to be, and then causes all to resolve back into its origin, spirit. Fohat is the absoluteness, the primal factor, and the sourcing beacon that will become all formed existence on all planes of expression. It is also the cause of form's demise. Fohat is Neptune, Uranus, Vulcan and Saturn combined. Neptune – the malleability of light and intrinsic purpose; Uranus – the shatterer, and the design, with one hand of magic reaching into heaven and one reaching down to earth; Vulcan – the fashioner of matter, the creator of beauty in form; and Saturn – the ring-pass-not of the limitation of sensed time and felt space, thus creating both the illusion and functionality of descent/ascent, embodiment/extrication, life and death. Saturn's limits create the sense of duality, and the ability through discipline to learn One.

Fohat, and the plane of Atma, are the Monad's breath expanding as it leaves the Source. Atma brings consciousness into a new way of Being.

---

[66] Rapport in French speaks of a mathematical relation, such as 1+1=2. This is incontrovertible. Buddhic rapport, likewise, is unquestionable, incontrovertible. Quality + energy = a specifically intended alchemical result.
[67] Of thought, pattern, or manifested substantial form.
[68] If our mind sees images of fire, we are not holding the consciousness in Atma. Image is naught on this plane. Image would be too formed and concept oriented.

Soul has been identified with matter and seeking to be more identified with spirit, yet it identified Self as middle, stretched between two worlds, a Savior to one, a Servant to the other. Atma provides identification *as*; as spirit – not apart from or a part of it. Atma provides identification as matter, densified spirit, perfect as form, law-fully representing the Grand Design of Life in all instances, through the veil of time/space.

To dare to enter Atma is to dare to Be. It is to dare to be Fohat, the spark of Life everywhere, and to know That to be the Identity of Self.

The Fifth Ray of Concrete Knowledge or Science and Initiates

To Reveal the Truth	brings	Illumination of Every Thing and Every One
Freedom of three levels of Mind	provide	Ability to implement the Ideas of God
Pure Mind	is	A Pure Channel for Divine Will[69]
To Unveil, Discover	is	To Understand that Love Underlies All
Understanding Method/Procedure	is	To Understand Manifestation in Matter
Clarity	provides	Being able to convey to others

Figure 35

Silence is Spirit when compared to anything other. Of course, that puts us back into the framework of duality. To be Silent is not just the obvious silence of those who "know but do not speak."[70] Disciples learn this rule of the Road early on. Reticence of speech, silence of the tongue is cultivated as the mind is stilled. At first it is an act of repression or suppression, but grows into a practice of stillness of thought, therefore less words. So much of our thought and speaking is harmful, selfish, and self-centered. We bind ourselves to possessions, fantasy, and dreams as we

---

[69] *Esoteric Psychology, Vol. I*, Pg. 76
[70] *The Tao te Ching*, verse 56. Translated by Stephen Mitchell. Harper and Row. 1988.

give voice to our desire nature countless times in our lives. The disciple learns when to speak and when not to. The initiate learns *how* to speak and when not to. The difference is efficacy. The initiate can wield power in word, thought, and action (seen or unseen by others), and so is responsible for all that he or she will put into action. The accountability is exact. Therefore, the initiate learns to use words of power and words as power within the planes of matter that all planes are. The white magician is the soul/spirit person. Her or his life is lived only to bring the fullest expression of matter to realization knowing that only thus is spiritualization fulfilled.

Silence, then, is the inner life of the initiate, living ever increasingly as spirit, the Soundless Sound, the Dark Light that is Life. Light fades as the initiate consciousness learns to reside in the atmic and monadic planes. Light is lived by consciousness. It is a manifestation of the Christ/Buddha principle within matter. Silence, or lack of sound, is an entering into communing versus communication. Silence absorbs the consciousness and adjusts it, overtaking its sense of individuality therefore duality, and holds it released from the confines and modifications of time/space. This is high nirvana or samadhi, but is not the bliss state of lower forms of conscious mind-full-ness (nirvana, samadhi, satori). Bliss is personal, dualistic. It is not identification.

Silence is a lack of friction, even the most refined forms of friction, like soul and mind, or buddhic rapport of quality and energy in geometric triangulation and workmanship. Silence is entering into the stream (the Tao) because it is spirit, the cause and source of consciousness; it is its completion. Monadic silence is full, stop, present, now.

Regarding the systemic laws we might look to the Law of Magnetic Control as it governs the control of the lower nature by that which is higher. And with this final law of the soul the Cosmic Law of Synthesis is very present. All becomes a synthesized whole, no longer the parts each demanding their self-determination. Instead, via Magnetic Control, resonance and shared life essence absorb the tendency of singularity and draw it into the coordination of the living whole. Like the four syllable AUM (fourth is the silence before or after), the form is only complete when all are functioning freely as the fulfillment of a greater whole.

The "Law of Free Standing" might be an appropriate second name for this law of the soul. The midway point is the ultimate asana. It is being able to stand free from the negative pulls of the below of matter and the equally negative isolation of asceticism pulling from above. Standing free, standing whole, and standing able, the initiate has stood the tests of time, elements, attractions, and illusions. Free, liberated, and ready, this person or group of people can stand as bridges or as supporting beams. Yet, they stand in the middle, involved in life not removed from it. They stand and work, serve, uplift, redeem. They stand and can radiate because they stand free.

Parting Thoughts

Each human being has the capacity to live more fully - more soulfully. As each person does so everything and everyone that is part of that person's life is affected. From the perspective of consciousness, this is a good thing.

Soul's work is to change whatever it can, to make use of appearance and form, and to reveal the Divine Impermanence of those same forms. The constant in life is consciousness and the light of it. From one lifetime to the next, it will be the consciousness (or mind to the Buddhists) that will survive, not our body or form.

The Seven Laws of the Soul clearly can be seen in our lives, in the life of the world, and in the creative processes put in motion by people growing in consciousness. This is magic in the world. Our mission, then, should we chose to accept it, is to grow, and grow the light that is in us, to be "a lamp unto ourselves" as the Buddha instructed, to be the "light of the world" as Christ told us, and to truly understand as the Sutras state "that all exists for the sake of the soul".

The Center for Esoteric Studies offers classes and programs in spiritual training. The Center comes to where the student body is located. Spirit Fire Meditative Retreat Center offers the same on campus in a retreat environment. Spirit Fire provides conference facilities to groups and corporate clients as well. Both organizations are educational, reaching out to the mind and heart of humanity at all levels.

Please contact us and join the corps of co-creators of light in the world.

center for esoteric studies
Liberating with Light

Spirit Fire
Meditative Retreat Center

www.CenterEsotericStudies.com
www.spiritfire.info

Glossary of Terms

Personality – the identity, the mask that an individual holds as his/her own. It is the coordinating principle of the three vehicles: mind, feelings, and physical body.

Soul- the Light within, the True Self, that is self-less, altruistic, and leads one into universal appreciation of life.

Monad – the Spirit of a human being. It is the source of Identity for a human. It is the cause of expression and the point of return.

Jiva – a Sanskrit terms for the conscious part of oneself. In other words, it is the amount of oneself that is conscious of being conscious. It is that which incarnates and grows lifetime to lifetime.

Astrality – sentiency, feelings, emotions, and desire within a life form, human or a member of another kingdom.

Fohat – a Sanskrit term for the primal or first impulse of dynamic life. It is the spark that self-contains all potential, the blueprints for design, structure, and completion, as well as the indicators of when to self-dissolve or destruct.

Appendix

A.

Psalm 23 reads, "The Lord is my shepherd, I shall not want. He maketh me to lie down in green pastures; he leadeth me beside still waters. He restoreth my soul; he leadeth me in the paths of righteousness for his namesake. Yea, though I walk through the valley of the shadow death, I will fear no evil; for thou art with me; thy rod and thy staff they comfort me. Thou preparest a table before me in the presence of mine enemies; thou anointest my head with oil; my cup runneth over. Surely goodness and mercy shall follow me all the days of my life; and I will dwell in the house of the Lord." *The Jerusalem Bible*. General editor, Alexander Jones. Doubleday & Company, 1966

B.

The Law of Sacrifice is the first law because all other laws of the soul are consequences of its enactment.

To sacrifice is to Serve.

To uplift and salvage is to move in Magnetic Impulse.

To recognize the needs of sacrifice is to Repulse.

Having done that we become a focal point of change and a point within Group Progress. All life then resonates to these points or seeds of liberation. Expansive Response is the resonance of spirit with spirit.

And the Law of the Lower Four gives us the measuring stick for freedom and the assurance of the reality of achievement via struggle and effort. Magic in the World Pg. 34

C.

Mantram of Service

May the peace and blessings of the Holy Ones pour forth over the worlds; Rest upon the work and the workers, protecting, purifying, energizing, and strengthening them.

There is a peace which passeth understanding;
It abides in the hearts of those who live in the eternal.
And there is a power which maketh all things new;
It lives and moves in those who know the self as One.

    D.
    Mantram of Unification

The sons of men are one and I am one with them.
I seek to love not hate.
I seek to serve and not exact due service.
I seek to heal not hurt.
Let pain bring due reward of light and love;
Let the soul control the outer form and life and all events
And bring to light the love that underlies the happenings of the time.
Let vision come and insight.
Let the future stand revealed.
Let inner union demonstrate and outer cleavages be gone.
Let love prevail. Let all men love.

Bibliography

Bailey, Alice A. *Esoteric Psychology, Vol. I*. New York: Lucis Publishing Company, 1984 (1936).

_____. *Esoteric Psychology, Vol. II*. New York: Lucis Publishing Company, 1981 (1942).

_____. *The Labours of Hercules*. New York: Lucis Publishing Company, 1974.

_____. *The Light of the Soul*. New York: Lucis Publishing Company, 1927.

_____. *A Treatise on White Magic*. New York: Lucis Publishing Company, 1980 (1934).

The Bhagavad Gita. Translated by Swami Nikhilananda. Ramakrishna-Vivekananda Center, New York, 1974.

Buddhists Texts Through the Ages. Translated and edited by Edward Conzel. Shambhala Publications, Inc., Boston, 1990.

Teachings of the Buddha. Edited by Jack Kornfield. Shambhala Publications, Inc., Boston, 1993.

The Jerusalem Bible. General editor, Alexander Jones. Doubleday & Company, 1966.

Tao Te Ching. Translated by Stephen Mitchell, Harper & Row Publishing, 1992.

Urantia. Urantia Foundation, Chicago, 1955.

Printed in the United States
967900005B